SECOND EDITION

IN CHARGE 1 WORKBOOK

An Integrated Skills Course for High-Level Students

Stephen Gudgel

Consulting authors
James E. Purpura
Diane Pinkley

LONGMAN ON THE WEB

Longman.com offers online resources for teachers and students. Access our Companion Websites, our online catalog, and our local offices around the world.

Longman English Success offers online courses to give learners flexible study options. Courses cover General English, Business English, and Exam Preparation.

Visit us at **longman.com** and **englishsuccess.com**.

Longman

In Charge 1 Workbook, Second Edition

Pearson Education, 10 Bank Street, White Plains, NY 10606

Vice president, director of publishing: Allen Ascher
Editorial manager: Pam Fishman
Project manager: Margaret Grant
Development editor: Debbie Lazarus
Vice president, director of design and production: Rhea Banker
Executive managing editor: Linda Moser
Production manager: Liza Pleva
Production editor/Reprint manager: Robert Ruvo
Director of manufacturing: Patrice Fraccio
Senior manufacturing buyer: Edie Pullman
Photo research: Jennifer McAliney
Cover design: Tracey Cataldo
Text composition: Design 5 Creatives
Text font: 11/14 Palatino
Illustrations: Larry Daste, pp. 1, 7, 11, 55, 68, 78; Susan Detrich, pp. 12, 19,
    26, 37, 38, 57, 65, 66, 70, 74; Tim Haggerty, pp. 52, 53, 74, 82; Andy Myer,
    p. 34; Larry Ross, pp. 28, 43, 44; Phil Scheuer, pp. 2, 3, 22, 30, 42, 49, 58,
    59, 83, 89
Photo credits: p. 5, ©Kevin R. Morris/CORBIS; p. 13, ©Bettmann/CORBIS;
    p. 21, ©AP/Wide World Photos; p. 35, ©AP/Wide World Photos; p. 45,
    ©Mimmo Jodice/CORBIS; p. 73, ©AP/Wide World Photos; p. 91, (t)
    ©AP/Wide World Photos; p. 91, (b) ©Japack Company/CORBIS
Text credits: p. 10, From SCHOLASTIC SCOPE, September 1997 issue.
    ©1997 by Scholastic Inc. Reprinted by permission of Scholastic Inc.

ISBN 0-13-094382-7

Printed in the United States of America
3 4 5 6 7 8 9 10-VHG-10 09 08 07

PRACTICE 1

A healthy diet contains servings from each food group. What do you eat in a typical day? Compare your daily food choices with a partner's. Use the food pyramid for reference.

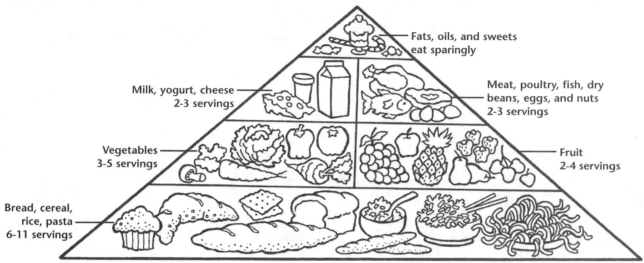

Fats, oils, and sweets
eat sparingly

Milk, yogurt, cheese
2-3 servings

Meat, poultry, fish, dry
beans, eggs, and nuts
2-3 servings

Vegetables
3-5 servings

Fruit
2-4 servings

Bread, cereal,
rice, pasta
6-11 servings

PRACTICE 2

Use the words in the box to complete the sentences.

blends	range
desirable	traced back to
delights in	resembles
mouth-watering	savor

1. Fusion cooking _____ spices, fruits, or vegetables from several cultures and cooks them together in a new way.

2. Many of our eating preferences can be _____ dishes our mothers served.

3. Look at the _____ desserts on that tray! Let's get one of each!

4. I hate to hurry in the morning; I need time to enjoy the morning paper as I _____ my first cup of coffee.

5. Though doctors love to tell us that drinking eight glasses of water each day is _____, I've never met anyone who actually does it!

6. Roberto _____ eating fruit from tropical countries. There are so many different varieties.

7. The taste of this vegetable _____ that of onion. What is it?

8. The new chef is skilled in making a wide _____ of dishes from different cultures.

PRACTICE 3

A. A sales clerk and a customer in a health food store are discussing various remedies. Work with a partner. Complete the conversation.

ROLES	CONVERSATION	FUNCTIONS
Customer:	Have you ever tried honey and lemon for a sore throat?	Ask about a remedy.
Sales clerk:	No, _____ _____	Answer the question.
Customer:	So what do you usually do for a sore throat?	Ask a follow-up question.
Sales clerk:	_____ _____	Answer the question and elaborate.

B. Take turns being the customer and the sales clerk and discuss other remedies.

    a. echinacea for a cold or flu   **c.** vitamin C for a cold

    b. ginseng tea for lack of energy   **d.** cucumber slices on tired eyes

PRACTICE 4

A group of students is taking a tour of a doughnut factory. Complete the conversation with the appropriate forms of the verbs in parentheses. In some cases, more than one answer is possible.

TOUR GUIDE: And now, if you **(1. follow)** _____ me, we'll begin our tour.

JAMAL: So when **(2. get)** _____ we _____ free samples of all the doughnuts?

TOUR GUIDE: I **(3. be)** _____ afraid that part **(4. come)** _____ later. Sorry!

JAMAL: I'll wait.

TOUR GUIDE: Well, here we are at the ingredients station. What you **(5. look)** _____ at now is the process of making raised doughnuts.

EMI: **(6. be)** _____ those the light, puffy kind?

TOUR GUIDE: Yes, they are. Here the machines **(7. add)** _____ yeast to the dough to make it rise. Then the batches of dough are set aside to go through one rising.

EMI: What **(8. happen)** _____ next?

TOUR GUIDE: Come over here. Do you see how those machines **(9. form)** _____ the dough into shapes and then **(10. drop)** _____ them into the hot oil vats?

JAMAL: Yeah. So the doughnuts **(11. fry)** _____ in there. It **(12. smell)** _____ delicious!

TOUR GUIDE: Yes, indeed. Now, over here, the machines **(13. decorate)** _____ newly fried doughnuts with toppings. See? They **(14. pour)** _____ on chocolate or strawberry or vanilla icing, **(15. dust)** _____ them with powdered sugar or colorful candy sprinkles . . .

JAMAL: I can't stand it any longer! I **(16. die)** _____! I **(17. beg)** _____ you! PLEASE give me a doughnut!

PRACTICE 5

Write the verbs in the correct column in the chart. Then choose two verbs from each column and write sentences on a separate sheet of paper.

appear	fry	grow	need	taste	think
cook	seem	look like	want	roast	feel
see	belong	boil	hear	know	steam

Action verbs	Stative verbs	Can be both

PRACTICE 6

Read each numbered sentence and check the statement that best describes it. Compare your answers with a partner's.

1. Joyce has been making pasta all afternoon.
   - ☐ She still has more pasta to make.
   - ☐ She has finished making all the pasta.

2. Bill's in great shape; he's been working out at the gym.
   - ☐ Bill used to work out at the gym.
   - ☐ Bill began working out and continues to do so.

3. Kim has never liked cooked carrots.
   - ☐ Kim didn't like cooked carrots but likes them now.
   - ☐ Kim didn't like cooked carrots in the past and doesn't like them now.

4. Sam has lived above the restaurant for seven years.
   - ☐ Sam lived above the restaurant and then moved.
   - ☐ Sam is still living above the restaurant.

5. My mother has been watching a lot of cooking shows and trying the recipes.
   - ☐ She watches a show and then tries a recipe.
   - ☐ She doesn't watch TV, so she has time to cook for us.

PRACTICE 7

Complete the passage with the appropriate form of the verbs in parentheses.
In some cases, more than one answer is possible.

One of the world's great staple foods, rice is a grain that
(1. belong) _____ to the grass family. The grain we
(2. know) _____ as rice **(3. come)** _____
from the flowers of the rice plant, which
(4. measure) _____ from .61 to 1.8
meters tall. Because rice **(5. need)** _____
warmth and moisture to grow, people on
every continent except Antarctica
(6. cultivate) _____ rice. Asian countries
(7. account for) _____ around 92 percent
of the world's rice production. Among these countries
are India, China, Japan, Indonesia, Thailand, Burma,
and Bangladesh. In recent years, these countries
(8. produce) _____ more than 550 million
tons of rice annually.

a rice paddy

Why **(9. be)** _____ rice _____ such an
essential food for more than two thirds of the world? To begin with, rice
(10. be) _____ one of the few foods in the world that is nonallergenic
and gluten-free. It **(11. contain)** _____ around 100 calories per
1/2 cup. In addition, there **(12. be)** _____ several varieties of grain,
each with its own distinctive length, texture, and taste.

Who **(13. not/hear)** _____ of the delicious Italian dish
known as risotto? It **(14. have)** _____ a wonderful
creamy texture and **(15. combine)** _____ perfectly with ingredients
such as mushrooms or asparagus. Another classic rice dish is rice pudding, which
people **(16. make)** _____ with different sweet ingredients for hundreds
of years. And we can't forget the wonderful rice dishes of China and Japan that
(17. gain) _____ such popularity the world over. And then there
(18. be) _____ paella from Spain and rice-stuffed grape leaves from
Greece and rice and beans from Mexico and pilaf from Turkey and curried rice
from India, to name just a few more world favorites. Rice? Nice!

PRACTICE 8

A. Before You Listen Discuss in small groups. What's your favorite dish? Do you know its origin? How is it prepared?

 B. Listen to an excerpt from a radio show devoted to food. Answer the questions. Then compare your answers with a partner's

1. What was the topic of today's show? _____.
2. What are the possible origins of pasta? _____.
3. What was the Etruscan evidence of pasta? _____.
4. How was pasta originally eaten? _____.
5. How was pasta cooked before the 18th century? _____.

C. Work with a partner. What new information about pasta did you learn? What are your favorite pasta dishes? What ingredients are used in them?

PRACTICE 9

A. Predict the pronunciation of the underlined words and write them in the correct column.

When we think of Indian food, we think of curry. The word we know as *curry* <u>derives</u> from the Tamil word *kari*, which <u>means</u> "sauce." Curry is not a single spice but rather a blend of <u>spices</u>. It typically <u>includes</u> coriander, cumin, fenugreek, turmeric, several <u>kinds</u> of pepper, cloves, cardamom, and cinnamon. The exact <u>ingredients</u> vary according to each cook, and recipes are highly guarded <u>secrets</u>. Curry <u>dishes</u> may be hot or mild, according to the <u>amounts</u> of the ingredients used.

/S/	/Z/	/IZ/
	derives	

 B. Listen to the paragraph to check your predictions.

PRACTICE 10

Work in small groups. Take turns opening a discussion on the following issues. Remember to follow these steps: greet, introduce, state the purpose, set a time frame, and open the discussion.

ISSUES

- Calcium is important in one's diet.
- Should children be forced to eat certain foods?
- Is fast food destroying cultural tradition?
- Men like meat, women like sweets.

PRACTICE 11

A. Read the text on yogurt. Underline the topic sentence of each paragraph. Then circle the sentences that support the main idea of each paragraph.

If there is such a thing as a wonder food, the creamy milk product known as yogurt would surely earn that name. Associated everywhere with long life, yogurt is nutritionally superior to ordinary milk in many ways. In fact, in many parts of the world such as southeastern Europe and Asia Minor, yogurt is the only form in which milk is consumed.

Used by many as a health food, the benefits of yogurt are almost limitless. Yogurt is an important source of calcium and vitamins, and if one to three cups of yogurt are eaten daily, some kinds of infection clear up quickly. Yogurt also aids in the digestion of iron. As a face mask, yogurt's astringent qualities are a help to oily skin.

Yogurt has become increasingly popular, and more and more people are interested in learning how to make it at home. To do so, heat one quart of fresh milk to "hand hot," about 110°F (43°C). To this very warm milk, add about three tablespoons of yogurt from a previous batch that contains live cultures (usually *Lactobacillus bulgaricus* and *Streptococcus thermophilus* or *Lactobacillus acidophilus*). Stir the mixture and pour it all at once into a wide-mouthed thermos jar. Cover it tightly and let it stand overnight. On uncapping the next morning, the yogurt will be thick and creamy. Refrigerate until served, and then enjoy.

B. What function and purpose does the writer have in mind? Check the boxes.

FUNCTION	**PURPOSE**
☐ Persuasion	☐ To inform
☐ Description	☐ To condemn

What would be a good title for this text?

_____

YOU'RE IN CHARGE!

UNIT ONE OBJECTIVES: How well did you meet the objectives for this unit? Check the box next to each objective you feel you mastered.

GRAMMAR
- ❏ Simple present tense
- ❏ Present progressive tense
- ❏ Present perfect tense
- ❏ Present perfect progressive tense

LISTENING
- ❏ Listening for gist
- ❏ Listening for details

SPEAKING
Opening a discussion
- ❏ Greetings
- ❏ Introductions
- ❏ Stating the purpose
- ❏ Setting a time frame
- ❏ Opening the discussion

PRONUNCIATION
- ❏ *–s* and *–es* endings in noun plurals and third-person singular verb forms

READING
Using context clues such as
- ❏ parts of speech
- ❏ prefixes, roots, suffixes
- ❏ synonyms and antonyms

WRITING
- ❏ Identifying parts of a paragraph
- ❏ Identifying parts of an essay
- ❏ Identifying topic, function, and purpose

LEARNING STRATEGIES: Reflect on your use of learning strategies and thinking skills in this unit. What are some of the strategies you employed? Which ones were most successful for you?

Write your thoughts here.

_____

_____

_____

_____

_____

_____

_____

_____

_____

Unit 1 Learning Strategies
- Using context to determine meaning
- Noting main ideas
- Noting details
- Brainstorming
- Classifying
- Taking notes
- Working cooperatively
- Using prior knowledge
- Skimming and scanning

PRACTICE 1

Celebrations are often memorable occasions. They can be personal, family, school, or work related. Work with a partner. Talk about special celebrations from your life.

- What were you celebrating?
- Where were you?
- How did you celebrate?
- Who participated in the celebrations?

PRACTICE 2

Complete the crossword puzzle. Refer to page 17 in your student book for help.

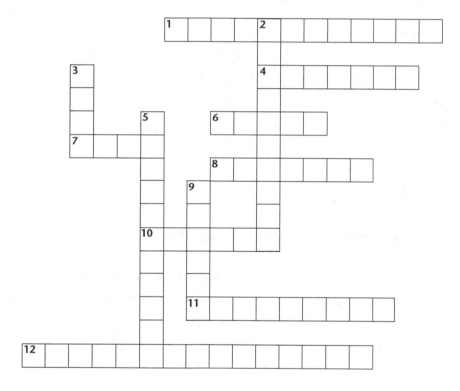

Across

1. others equivalent in function
4. mainly, mostly
6. having skill and ability
7. exchange
8. newly created
10. attracts attention, is interesting
11. made-up stories
12. direct, honest

Down

2. hidden
3. therefore
5. progressing, likely to succeed
9. start, begin

PRACTICE 3

A. An editor and a journalist are talking about some of the big events of the past few years. Work with a partner and complete the conversation.

ROLES	CONVERSATION	FUNCTIONS
Editor:	What were some of the big events from the last few years that you remember?	Ask about memorable events.
Journalist:	Well, I remember _____ _____	Give information about a past event.
Editor:	Were you there? _____ _____	Ask for details.
Journalist:	_____ _____	Elaborate.
Editor:	_____ _____	Make a closing comment.

B. Take turns being the editor and the journalist and discuss these other memorable events.

a. World Cup soccer finals
b. summer and winter Olympics
c. World Trade Center attack, Sept. 11, 2001
d. Nelson Mandela becomes president of South Africa
e. a major earthquake

PRACTICE 4

A. Complete the passage with the appropriate form of the verbs in parentheses. In some cases, more than one answer is possible.

The writer Victor Martínez didn't have an easy childhood. His parents were migrant laborers. While many children (**1. play**) _____ with their friends, Martínez (**2. spend**) _____ his days in the hot fields. When he (**3. be**) _____ a baby, his mother (**4. leave**) _____ him in the car while she (**5. pick**) _____ tomatoes, grapes, peaches, chiles, and cotton. As soon as he was able to help in the fields, he (**6. begin**) _____ to pick crops too. In fact, the work became such a part of him that it invaded his dreams. One night his parents (**7. wake up**) _____ at 3:00 A.M. and found that Victor was not in his bed. They (**8. go**) _____ outside to see what (**9. happen**) _____. Young Victor (**10. pick**) _____ grapes! He (**11. have**) _____ a metal pan and a knife and (**12. cut**) _____ the grapes off the vine and (**13. put**) _____ them into the pan. He (**14. sleep walk**) _____.

B. Compare your answers with a partner's and explain your choices.

PRACTICE 5

A. Practice the conversation with a partner.

> **A:** Who *invented* the first steam engine?
>
> **B:** I believe it was James Watt in 1769.
>
> **A:** Yes, he was the official inventor, but Thomas Savery and Thomas Newcomen *had already invented* simpler forms of steam power.

B. Use the information from the chart to create new conversations about inventions and discoveries.

Invention or Discovery	Recognized Inventor	Previously
Steam engine	James Watt 1769	Thomas Savery in 1698 and Thomas Newcomen in 1712 invented earlier, simpler forms of steam power.
Dynamo principle	Michael Faraday 1831	Study of electricity began in the early 1600s.
First official telegraph line and Morse code	Samuel F. B. Morse 1843	Prototype for telegraph existed in early nineteenth century.
Radio communications technology	Guglielmo Marconi 1895—built a radio transmitter and receiver	Heinrich Hertz generated and detected the first known radio waves in 1888.
Penicillin	Alexander Fleming 1928	Ernest Duchesne found a mold that seemed to kill bacteria in 1896.

PRACTICE 6

Correct the verb tense errors in the sentences. Cross out the incorrect words and write the corrections above the verbs.

1. When Christopher Columbus ~~had sailed~~ *sailed* across the Atlantic, he ~~looked~~ *was looking* for the East Indies, but he landed in the Bahamas.

2. When Benjamin Franklin flew a kite, he was discovering that lightning was a form of electricity.

3. Before they were developing the first powered heavier-than-air aircraft, the Wright Brothers had flown gliders.

4. Scottish inventor Alexander Graham Bell worked on ways to improve the telegraph when he invented the telephone.

5. Sometime around 1450, while a German goldsmith named Johannes Gutenberg had studied several key printing technologies, he created a hand-operated mechanical printing press.

A. Complete the sentences with the appropriate form of the verbs in parentheses. In some cases, more than one answer is possible.

1. The Mexican Revolution (**begin**) _____ in 1810 while Napoleon's brother was on the throne of Spain.

2. When Matthew Henson (**accompany**) _____ Lt. Peary to the North Pole, he became the first African American to explore that region.

3. While the French (**fight**) _____ the British in 1800, Robert Fulton unsuccessfully tried to sell them his submarine, the *Nautilus*.

4. Gandhi (**practice**)_____ nonviolent civil disobedience while pursuing India's independence.

5. While still a teenager, Joan of Arc (**lead**) _____ armies to defeat the English.

6. When Simon Bolívar (**fight**) _____ the Spanish forces in 1819 at Boyacá, he successfully surprised and defeated them.

7. The British ship Titanic (**sink**) _____ on the night of April 14, 1912, when it crashed into an iceberg in the north Atlantic Ocean.

8. By the age of three, Tiger Woods (**appear**) _____ on TV talk shows.

B. Compare your answers with a partner's and explain your choices.

A. **Before You Listen** Discuss in small groups. What does courage mean to you? Do you know someone who is courageous? Share something about that person.

B. Listen to this interview about the life of a major league baseball player. Answer the questions.

Jackie Robinson

1. When and where was Jackie Robinson born? _____

_____

2. Which college sports did he play? _____

_____

3. Where did he play for the Monarchs? _____

_____

4. What historical event did he bring about? _____

_____

5. How did he show courage? _____

_____

6. What awards did he win? _____

_____

7. When did Robinson retire from baseball? _____

_____

C. Work with a partner. Compare your answers and take turns retelling the major events of Jackie Robinson's life. Use time expressions such as *first, next, then,* and *finally.*

PRACTICE 9

A. Predict the ending sound of the italicized word in each sentence and write the sound /d/, /Id/, or /t/ on the line.

_____ **1.** The first cable TVs *appeared* in rural areas of the United States in 1948.

_____ **2.** Brazilians consider tennis star Gustavo Kuerten as a *blessed* hero.

_____ **3.** Women *competed* in the Olympic Games for the first time in 1900.

_____ **4.** Charles Lindbergh's first transatlantic flight in 1927 gave a much-*needed* boost to air travel.

_____ **5.** In 1968, Shirley Chisholm was the first African American woman *elected* to the U.S. Congress.

_____ **6.** The first Native American newspaper, the "Cherokee Phoenix", was *published* in 1828.

_____ **7.** Albert Einstein was a *learned* physicist who had learning difficulties early in his school career.

_____ **8.** In 1932, Amelia Earhart was the first woman pilot who *crossed* the Atlantic Ocean alone.

B. Listen to the sentences to check your predictions.

C. Work with a partner and take turns reading the sentences.

PRACTICE 10

A. Work with a partner. Take turns defining the following issues as you perceive them. Use the language for defining issues from the box.

> **Useful Language for Defining Issues**
>
> As I see it, the real issue here is . . .   I'm talking about . . .
> I mean . . .   When I say . . .

ISSUES

• Young people who are seriously involved in sports face all kinds of pressure.

• The fact that people live longer creates new challenges in health care.

• Our existing natural resources are getting scarce.

Read the topic sentences and write a possible essay question for each one. Check whether your essay question is for a persuasive or descriptive essay.

Example:

TOPIC SENTENCE: People attend colleges or universities for many different reasons. One important reason is to gain the knowledge that is needed for a future career.

ESSAY QUESTION: *People go to college or university for many different reasons. What are some of the reasons? Give specific examples for each reason you mention.*

☐ Persuasive
☑ Descriptive

1. **TOPIC SENTENCE:** Some community members would like to see the XYZ Company build a new factory in our community. They think it will offer more employment opportunities. However, I believe that XYZ Company should not be allowed into our community. They already have a reputation for polluting the nearby waterways.

Possible Essay Question:

_____

_____

☐ Persuasive

☐ Descriptive

2. **TOPIC SENTENCE:** In some countries, teenagers are allowed and even encouraged to work while they attend school. I believe this is a good idea. In fact, I think all students should combine work and school as a regular routine.

Possible Essay Question:

_____

_____

☐ Persuasive

☐ Descriptive

3. **TOPIC SENTENCE:** Fifty years ago, people were not expected to live as long as they are living today. Life expectancy has increased for several reasons.

Possible Essay Question:

_____

_____

☐ Persuasive

☐ Descriptive

YOU'RE IN CHARGE!

UNIT TWO OBJECTIVES: How well did you meet the objectives for this unit? Check the box next to each objective you feel you mastered.

GRAMMAR	**LISTENING**	**SPEAKING**
❑ Simple past tense ❑ Past progressive tense ❑ Past perfect tense	❑ Listening for sequence of events	❑ Defining the issue

PRONUNCIATION	**READING**	**WRITING**
❑ *–ed* endings of past tense verbs and *–ed* verb forms used as adjectives	❑ Reading for time organization	❑ Analyzing essay questions

LEARNING STRATEGIES: Reflect on your use of learning strategies and thinking skills in this unit. What are some of the strategies you employed? Which ones were most successful for you?

Write your thoughts here.

_____

_____

_____

_____

_____

_____

_____

_____

_____

Unit 2 Learning Strategies
- Using context to determine meaning
- Using graphic organizers
- Noting details
- Brainstorming
- Classifying
- Taking notes
- Working cooperatively
- Analyzing
- Using prior knowledge
- Skimming and scanning

PRACTICE 1

Work with a partner. Look at the directors and their movies and answer the questions.

Directors and Their Movies

Spike Lee — *Malcolm X*

Ang Lee — *Crouching Tiger, Hidden Dragon*

Majid Majidi — *The Children of Heaven*

George Lucas — *Star Wars*

Yimou Zhang — *Raise the Red Lantern*

Steven Spielberg — *Jurassic Park*

Carlos Saura — *Tango*

Jane Campion — *The Piano*

Akira Kurosawa — *Seven Samurai*

Walter Salles — *Central Station*

- What countries are these directors from?
- Which ones do you know and which ones do you like?
- Which directors do you think will become more popular in the future?

PRACTICE 2

Use the words in the box to complete the sentences.

---

deliver	hubs
pristine	spools
encrypted	screening

---

1. We found about thirty _____ of old home movies in our grandparents' attic.

2. Be careful with this DVD. It is loaded with _____ information.

3. Digital data is often transmitted to regional

   _____ that in turn send it out to smaller computer networks.

4. We called the video rental company and asked them to _____

   two movies to us on Friday.

5. Antonio Banderas's family went to the _____ of his film *Crazy in Alabama*.

6. In *A River Runs Through It*, we can see the _____ rivers and lakes of Montana.

PRACTICE 3

A. A man and woman are in line to buy tickets for the movies. Work with a partner. Complete the conversation.

ROLES	CONVERSATION	FUNCTIONS
Man:	What do you think will be the future for female directors?	Ask for a prediction.
Woman:	In my opinion, _____ _____ _____	Make a prediction.
Man:	Why is that?	Ask for a reason.
Woman:	Because _____ _____ _____	Give a reason.

B. Take turns being the man and woman and make other predictions.

a. movie stars as directors   **d.** violence in movies

b. censorship of movies   **e.** movies about social change

c. number of independent movies (not produced in Hollywood)   **f.** (your own idea)

PRACTICE 4

A. Complete the conversation with an appropriate form of the verbs in parentheses. In some cases, more than one answer is possible.

JAIME: Hello.

PEPE: Hi. Could I speak to Jaime, please?

JAIME: Speaking.

PEPE: Oh, hi Jaime. It's Pepe.

JAIME: Pepe! It's great to hear from you. What's going on?

PEPE: Well, I was wondering what you (**1. do**) _____ on Saturday night?

JAIME: Ummm . . . Actually I (**2. attend**) _____ the premiere of the movie *Ice Age* with Carmen and Paulino. I'm sure it (**3. be**) _____ good.

PEPE: Oh, I've heard that too. Gee, I wish I could go.

JAIME: It's by invitation only, but I can probably get another ticket if you want to join us. I (**4. call**)_____ and see if I can get you an invitation.

PEPE: That would be great. What time (**5. it / start**) _____? And where (**6. it / play**)_____?

JAIME: I think it (**7. start**) _____ at 8:00, but I (**8. check**) _____ to be sure. It (**9. play**) _____ at that nice art deco theater, the Lorraine.

PEPE: Okay, well, I (**10. go**) _____ as long as you can get the invitation for me. How (**11. you / get**) _____ to the Lorraine? It's pretty far.

JAIME: You're right, and as usual, we still haven't decided. Carmen wants to drive, Paulino wants to go by bus, and I can't decide what I want to do. Wait, I know! We (**12. hail**) _____ a cab and pick you up on our way. How's that?

PEPE: Great! I hope you get that invitation. If so, I (**13. see**) _____ you all on Saturday.

JAIME: Okay. I (**14. call**) _____ you back and tell you what I found out. Bye, Pepe.

PEPE: Bye. And thanks.

B. Compare your answers with a partner's and explain your choices.

PRACTICE 5

A. You are planning a camping trip this weekend with Su Li. Complete the e-mail message on the next page with appropriate future forms of the verbs in the box.

go	take	leave	wait	talk	be	bring

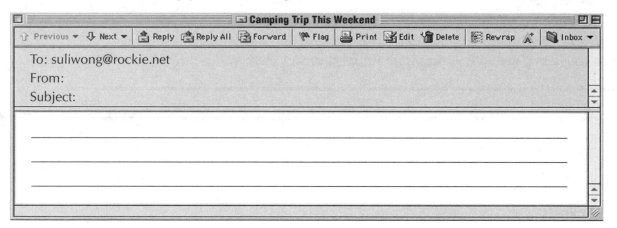

Camping Trip This Weekend

Previous ▼ Next ▼ | Reply Reply All Forward | Flag | Print Edit Delete | Rewrap A⁺ | Inbox ▼

To:
From: suliwong@rockie.net
Re: Camping Trip This Weekend

Hi!

_____ we still _____ camping this weekend? I hope so. I

watched the weather predictions on TV and they say it _____ nice and fairly

warm. That's good news! What _____ with you for the weekend? I think I

_____ jeans and sweatshirts to wear at night and shorts and t-shirts to wear

during the daytime. I _____ my hiking boots, but no other shoes. What time

_____we _____ town? What time _____ you

_____ work? _____ you _____ your car, for

sure? I hope so, because mine needs to be taken to the garage before I drive very far. I

_____ for a message from you tomorrow. I _____ to you soon!

Su Li

B. Now write a short reply to the message.

Camping Trip This Weekend

Previous ▼ Next ▼ | Reply Reply All Forward | Flag | Print Edit Delete | Rewrap A⁺ | Inbox ▼

To: suliwong@rockie.net
From:
Subject:

_____

_____

_____

PRACTICE 6

Listen to five conversations. Put the number of the conversation in the box next to its purpose.

PURPOSE

☐ **a.** buying movie tickets

☐ **b.** making a complaint

☐ **c.** asking about opening
   and closing times

☐ **d.** getting information about services

☐ **e.** making a reservation

PRACTICE 7

A. Before You Listen Discuss with a partner. Do you often watch films in another language with subtitles? How often? What advantages do films in the original language have? What disadvantages?

movie poster advertising Titanic

🎧 **B.** Listen to an interview with a film commentator. Number the predictions in the order you hear them made.

_____ **a.** "North American directors are going to realize that they also need to change their mindset and have native dialogue in their films."

_____

_____

_____ **b.** "We're going to discover more great Chinese directors, actors, and movies."

_____

_____

_____ **c.** "More and more people in the U.S. are going to be open to viewing subtitled movies."

_____

_____

_____ **d.** "I think we'll see a lot more films from other countries."

_____

_____

C. Listen again. What information can be used to support the predictions? Write the supporting information on the lines under each prediction.

D. Work with a partner and compare your answers.

PRACTICE 8

A. Predict the stress of each underlined word. Put an accent mark on the stressed syllable.

1. We went to the <u>produce</u> department of the supermarket.
   Woody Allen is going to <u>produce</u> another new film soon.

2. On Friday, John Woo will <u>address</u> a film study group in Mexico City.
   I'm going to look up the <u>address</u> of Universal Studios.

3. The lead actor could possibly <u>contract</u> a disease while on location.
   Penelope Cruz is going to sign a new <u>contract</u>.

4. They will shoot their next film in the <u>desert</u>.
   The dissatisfied actors were ready to <u>desert</u> the production.

5. Samira Makhmalbaf was the <u>object</u> of a lot of attention in Cannes.
   Censors didn't <u>object</u> to the harsh language of the film.

6. The new director's work will <u>progress</u> very quickly.
   Our new movie has been making a lot of <u>progress</u>.

B. Listen to the sentences to check your predictions.

C. Work with a partner and take turns reading the sentences.

PRACTICE 9

Work with a partner. Each take one side of the argument for or against censorship of movies. Brainstorm five good reasons for your side. Use the expressions on the next page for arguing and counterarguing.

For Movie Censorship

Some people feel that movies should provide good role models and that vice, dishonesty, corruption, sex, bigotry, and other things they feel are bad examples for the viewers should be censored.

Against Movie Censorship

Some people feel that censorship is wrong and that people who make movies should be able to do so in complete freedom. After all, the public can decide for themselves whether to attend a movie or not.

USEFUL LANGUAGE

Arguing	**Counterarguing**
You have to admit that . . .	<u>Contradictions</u>
You must agree that . . .	Not at all . . .
Don't you think/agree that . . . ?	Quite the opposite: . . .
Clearly, . . .	Actually, that's not accurate/true: . . .
You can't deny that . . .	<u>Concessions</u>
The fact is that . . .	Yes, but still, . . .
The facts show that . . .	Maybe so, but . . .
	Even so, . . .
	Even if that's true, . . .

PRACTICE 10

Write a short persuasive composition for or against censorship in movies. Begin by writing your introduction below and sharing it with a partner.

_____

_____

_____

_____

_____

_____

_____

_____

_____

YOU'RE IN CHARGE!

UNIT THREE OBJECTIVES: How well did you meet the objectives for this unit? Check the box next to each objective you feel you mastered.

GRAMMAR Future meaning using ❑ will ❑ be going to ❑ simple present ❑ present progressive	**LISTENING** ❑ Evaluating arguments	**SPEAKING** ❑ Arguing for a position ❑ Arguing against a positon ❑ Offering concessions
PRONUNCIATION ❑ Stress patterns for two syllable nouns/verbs such as **con**trast/con**trast**	**READING** ❑ Assessing strengths and weaknesses of examples	**WRITING** Analyzing a persuasive essay ❑ introduction ❑ thesis statement ❑ arguments for and against ❑ supporting examples ❑ conclusion

LEARNING STRATEGIES: Reflect on your use of learning strategies and thinking skills in this unit. What are some of the strategies you employed? Which ones were most successful for you?

Write your thoughts here.

_____

_____

_____

_____

_____

_____

_____

_____

_____

_____

_____

Unit 3 Learning Strategies
- Using context to determine meaning
- Noting details
- Taking notes
- Using prior knowledge
- Working cooperatively
- Classifying
- Recognizing examples
- Evaluating information
- Brainstorming
- Making predictions

PRACTICE 1

Work with a partner and discuss the questions.

- Have you ever had a conflict with anyone from the box?
- Who was your most recent conflict with? What happened?
- How was it resolved?

a coworker	a classmate	a business partner	a good friend
a teacher	your boss	a teammate	a stranger in line
a shop clerk	a police officer	a spectator at a game	a family member

PRACTICE 2

Match the definitions with the vocabulary words from page 44 in your student book.
Then find and circle those five words in the puzzle.

```
V G S T R I V E T E W E C V X
C K R H A S V N D I I S O U C
G A S I M N E R L T R I N F A
L C F K E M T L X E K U F O N
N F L P U V I H S L D G L U T
D X F G W N A O E D U S I V H
M B R R G O L N T L V I C B E
X A E N N V T G C N P D T T L
H D E V E A N W S E A Q M F P
T S U R V A L I D A T E S K E
S P Y E M P A T H I Z E Z R V
L H U O E O Z G I L F X N Q T
```

1. hide, cover

   _____

2. complaint

   _____

3. be unable to avoid

   _____

4. confirm as true

   _____

5. put yourself in another person's
   position

   _____

PRACTICE 3

A. Work with a partner. Write a conversation about one of the situations. Use the chart to guide you.

Situation 1:

Your boyfriend/girlfriend thinks you have been spending too much time with other people and wants you to spend more time together. You want time to be with your friends. Tell a close friend about this problem.

Situation 2:

You wore your brother's new jacket to a party and left it on the bus. Your brother is furious. Tell a friend about this problem.

Roles	Conversation	Functions
You:	_____	Talk about a conflict.
Friend:	_____	Express understanding and ask for more information.
You:	_____	Explain the circumstance.
Friend:	_____	Give advice.
You:	_____	Respond to the advice.

B. Take turns with the roles. Share your conversation with the class.

A. Amelia has had a fight with her roommate, Marina, and has written her a letter. Complete the letter with the appropriate form of the verbs in parentheses.

Dear Marina,

I have put off **(1. write)** _____ this letter because I hardly know where to begin. I really dislike **(2. have)** _____ conflicts and would like **(3. avoid)** _____
(4. have) _____ this one. I would prefer
(5. talk) _____ about this in person, but I know it's difficult right now.

I don't want to blame you for **(6. ruin)** _____ my sweater. I realize that we can't help **(7. have)** _____ accidents and I know you didn't intend **(8. do)** _____ anything wrong. I had considered **(9. not say)** _____ anything to you about it, to keep from **(10. have)** _____ a confrontation, but I found I couldn't, because I am too upset.

It's just that this particular sweater has sentimental value. My grandmother made it for me just before she died. I have enjoyed **(11. wear)** _____ it and **(12. remember)** _____ my wonderful grandmother.

There is nothing you can do about it now. I will get over it. It couldn't last forever and, of course, a valuable friend is more important than a sweater. Just please agree **(13. be)** _____ more careful with my things in the future. I'm sorry I lost my temper. Sometimes I can't help **(14. overreact)** _____.

See you tonight.

Your friend,
Amelia

B. Discuss with a partner. What do you think happened with Amelia's sweater? How would you have handled the situation if you were Amelia?

PRACTICE 5

Work with a partner. Write a brief conversation using the verbs in the box. Develop your conversation around one of the situations. Then share it with the class.

Example:

Verbs	
fail	can't help
expect	would hate
appreciate	dislike
blame (someone) for	consider
deny	persuade
prevent (someone) from	
criticize (someone) for	

SITUATIONS
- Your teacher gave you a bad grade.
- Your best friend forgot to meet you.
- Your roommate didn't give you an important phone message.

PRACTICE 6

A. Correct any mistakes **after** the underlined expressions. Find eight more mistakes.

to speak

TEACHER: I'd **(1.)** <u>like</u> ~~speaking~~ to you about the analytical essay you handed in for homework last week.

STUDENT: Yes, I **(2.)** <u>volunteered</u> doing it for extra credit, remember?

TEACHER: Oh, that's right. Well, I can't give you the extra credit. In fact, I **(3.)** <u>refuse</u> to accept your essay at all.

STUDENT: Why is that?

TEACHER: What you wrote actually came from a student I had last year. I **(4.)** <u>managed</u> finding his paper in my files. I knew when I read your essay that it sounded familiar. At first, I **(5.)** <u>hesitated</u> to think such a thing, but after I **(6.)** <u>kept on</u> to read, I saw that your essay was exactly the same as his. Do you **(7.)** <u>deny</u> to copy the essay exactly as someone else wrote it?

STUDENT: I'm not going to **(8.)** <u>deny</u> doing that. I thought I **(9.)** <u>could prevent</u> to fail your course by doing extra work.

TEACHER: Extra work is fine as long as it's **your** extra work and not someone else's.

STUDENT: I understand. I'm very sorry. I hope you'll **(10.)** <u>forgive me for</u> to make such a mistake. Can I **(11.)** <u>persuade you</u> letting me try again with my own words this time?

TEACHER: All right. I'll **(12.)** <u>permit you</u> trying one more time, but I'll be looking at it very closely.

B. Compare your answers with a partner's. Discuss your opinion about the student's and teacher's actions.

PRACTICE 7

A. **Before You Listen** Discuss with a partner. What are the differences between the conflict resolution styles in the box?

B. Listen to the conversations. Match these styles with the conversations.

CONVERSATION 1 _____

CONVERSATION 2 _____

CONVERSATION 3 _____

C. Work with a partner. Discuss how you would have resolved these conflicts.

PRACTICE 8

A. Predict which words will be stressed in the sentences and underline them.

1. No, I didn't say you had it. I said Hugh had it!
2. Was that 13 centimeters or 30 centimeters?
3. Not a complaint from a resident. It's a complaint from the president.
4. Do you think that was a win-lose or a win-win resolution?
5. No, it wasn't last night. It's tomorrow night.
6. She didn't buy a sheep farm. She bought a cheap farm and then had problems.
7. Did you say I could eat for three or for free?
8. No, the house wasn't Ruby's. It was Rudy's.

B. Listen to the sentences to check your predictions.

C. Work with a partner and take turns reading the sentences.

PRACTICE 9

A. Read these sentences of disagreement. Write **I** (impolite) or **P** (polite).

_____ **1.** Yeah, I understand that you really like it there, but . . .

_____ **2.** I don't want you to feel cramped, but if you could only move your seat half-way.

_____ **3.** You can't prevent people from being comfortable just so that you can work.

_____ **4.** You should be in first class if you have work to take care of.

_____ **5.** Well, it tastes different, but variations can be nice.

_____ **6.** I'd like to help you, but I hate giving up a seat I've specifically chosen.

_____ **7.** I don't know what makes you think it's _your_ seat.

_____ **8.** I can't believe the way you acted at that party!

B. Compare your answers with a partner's. Discuss how you could change the impolite statements to polite ones.

PRACTICE 10

Work with a partner. Read the situations on the next page and choose one to act out. Use the language in the box to help.

Useful Language

I guess maybe I (was/did) . . .

I can agree with you, at least partially, but . . .

I may be wrong, but . . .

I hate to contradict you, but . . .

I am trying to see it from your perspective.

I'm sorry but that's not how I see it.

Could we look for a compromise?

O.K., I see your point, however . . .

To a certain point I agree with you . . .

SITUATION 1: Buying bus tickets for a bus that leaves in ten minutes

    Role A: A person tries to get in front of you in the line to buy tickets. Politely resolve the disagreement.

    Role B: The person behind you accuses you of jumping in front of him or her in the line. Politely resolve the disagreement.

SITUATION 2: Meeting to discuss job performance

    Role A: You are the boss and don't feel that this employee deserves a good evaluation or a raise. Explain your position politely.

    Role B: Your boss tells you that he or she is not pleased with your job performance. You are not getting the raise you think you deserve. Politely disagree with your boss.

PRACTICE 11

A. Look at the topic suggestions for a short composition. Write each topic under the appropriate heading in the chart. Then discuss your answers in small groups.

TOPIC SUGGESTIONS

- Conflict Resolution
- The Most Effective Style for Conflict Resolution
- My Personal Experience with a Cross-Cultural Conflict
- Understanding People from Different Cultures
- Mediation as One Means of Conflict Resolution
- Problems Among Students

Topic Is Too Broad	Topic Is Appropriate and Specific

B. Choose one of the appropriate and specific topics and write a short composition. Remember to include a thesis statement and supporting information.

YOU'RE IN CHARGE!

UNIT FOUR OBJECTIVES: How well did you meet the objectives for this unit? Check the box next to each objective you feel you mastered.

GRAMMAR	**LISTENING**	**SPEAKING**
❑ Gerunds or infinitives following a verb ❑ *it* + infinitive or *it* + adjective + infinitive	❑ Applying background knowledge	❑ Managing conflict

PRONUNCIATION	**READING**	**WRITING**
❑ Contrastive stress patterns	❑ Evaluating points of view	❑ Choosing and narrowing a topic

LEARNING STRATEGIES: Reflect on your use of learning strategies and thinking skills in this unit. What are some of the strategies you employed? Which ones were most successful for you?

Write your thoughts here.

_____

_____

_____

_____

_____

_____

_____

_____

_____

Unit 4 Learning Strategies
- Categorizing
- Using prior knowledge
- Using context to determine meaning
- Noting details
- Brainstorming
- Comparing
- Working cooperatively
- Making predictions

PRACTICE 1

Work in small groups. Look at the imaginary jobs titles in the box and discuss what these people do for a living. Be creative and make the job as unusual as possible.

Example: A revegetator recycles fruit and vegetables.

ringwarmer	dimensionologist	revegetator
midnightist	glassglider	carpetpooler

PRACTICE 2

Use the words in the box to complete the sentences.

1. My partner and I wanted to have a new experience so we decided to go for lessons and learn to _____.

2. The first thing we had to do was go to a sports shop and _____.

3. The training center is near where we live, so it's _____.

4. When we went up for the first time, my partner got scared and was ready to _____.

5. When you see all those people jumping out of planes, it's easy to _____ on all the excitement.

6. Many people said that to jump with a parachute you have to be a _____.

7. So far, I have seven jumps _____.

back out
convenient
get hooked
under my belt
skydive
daredevil
gear up

PRACTICE 3

Two friends who haven't seen each other for a long time suddenly meet. Yoko asks Jim about his job. Work with a partner. Complete the conversation and take turns practicing each role.

ROLES	CONVERSATION	FUNCTIONS
Yoko:	What type of _____?	Ask about a job.
Jim:	I'm a _____.	Name the job.
Yoko:	Really? That sounds_____. What kind of experience and education _____?	Comment and ask for details.
Jim:	Well, you need a university education and _____.	Explain about the job.
Yoko:	And what's your favorite aspect _____?	Ask for more information.
Jim:	Well, I'd have to say it's _____.	Elaborate.

PRACTICE 4

A. Complete the passage with the appropriate form of the verbs in parentheses.

When a passenger's luggage **(1. lose)** <u>is lost</u>, the lost luggage locator goes into action.

First, a lost luggage claim form has to **(2. fill out)** _____ by the passenger. A full description of each piece of luggage **(3. _modal_, give)** _____ and a picture from a list of pictures of different luggage types **(4. _modal_, choose)** _____ to provide the locator with as much information as possible. The contents of the luggage **(5. list)** _____ so that badly damaged luggage **(6. _modal_, identify)** _____ from the contents.

Next, the information on the ticket **(7. check)** _____ against the information on the claim form to be sure that the routing information is correct. Then the information **(8. enter)** _____ in the computer. Later, a printout **(9. prepare)** _____ that shows each place this luggage **(10. send)** _____ from the time it **(11. check in)** _____ at the airport.

The passenger **(12. hand)** _____ a claim ticket and **(13. ask)** _____ for a telephone number where he/she **(14. _modal_, reach)** _____ and an address where the luggage **(15. _modal_, deliver)** _____ when it **(16. find)** _____ .

B. Work with a partner. Compare your answers and explain your choices.

PRACTICE 5

A. Read these sentences describing odd jobs. Write the sentences in the passive voice.

> **Example:** You learn the gestures and voice of the famous person.
> _The gestures and voice of the famous person are learned._

1. You buy gifts and items for busy people.

_____

2. You make beautiful sculptures from simple balloons.

_____

making balloon sculptures

3. In film work, you give assistance and support to the
gaffer (electrical specialist).

_____

4. You test products to make sure they work.

_____

5. You provide services for people who don't have time to walk their dogs.

_____

6. You direct the circus show and announce the acts.

_____

7. You sample the food at the local restaurants and write a review.

_____

B. Compare your sentences with a partner's. Then match the sentence numbers with the jobs in the box.

> _____ balloon artist   _____ ringmaster
> _____ restaurant critic   _____ best boy
> _____ product tester   _____ celebrity impersonator
> _____ dog walker   _____ professional shopper

PRACTICE 6

Read each numbered sentence and check the statement that best describes it.

1. Dangerous jobs such as truck driver, forest fire fighter, and construction worker attract certain kinds of people.

   ☐ Certain kinds of people are attracted by dangerous jobs such as truck driver, forest fire fighter, and construction worker.

   ☐ Certain kinds of people will be attracted by dangerous jobs such as truck driver, forest fire fighter, and construction worker.

2. Working outdoors increases the level of risk and injury on the job.

   ☐ Working outdoors has increased the level of risk and injury on the job.

   ☐ The level of risk and injury on the job is increased by working outdoors.

3. Workers who have outdoor jobs will be affected by severe weather conditions.

   ☐ Severe weather conditions have affected workers who have outdoor jobs.

   ☐ Severe weather conditions will affect workers who have outdoor jobs.

4. For example, bad weather can cause a higher rate of fishers drowning.

   ☐ For example, a higher rate of fishers drowning can be caused by bad weather.

   ☐ For example, a higher rate of fishers drowning will cause bad weather.

5. Taxi driver has been reported as a dangerous job by the U.S. Labor Department.

   ☐ The U. S. Labor Department has reported taxi driver as a dangerous job.

   ☐ The U. S. Labor Department will report taxi driver as a dangerous job.

6. Does the thought of dangerous work excite you?

   ☐ Was the exitement of dangerous work thought by you?

   ☐ Are you excited by the thought of dangerous work?

PRACTICE 7

A. **Before You Listen** Discuss with a partner. What do you think of when you hear "master water taster"? What would a master water taster do? What does good water taste like?

B. Listen to the lecture on water tasting. List the four steps in the water tasting process.

1. _____

2. _____

3. _____

4. _____

C. Listen again and make notes on specific information you hear or can infer in the three categories.

About Smell	About Swallowing Water	About Taste

D. Work with a partner and compare your answers. Then take turns retelling the tap water tasting process using the steps you've written and the information from the chart.

PRACTICE 8

A. Predict the stress pattern of the compound words in the following sentences. Circle the syllables in the underlined words that receive the primary stress.

1. I'd love to be a (res)taurant critic. I love to eat!

2. Diane could never be a <u>wedding planner</u>. Weddings always make her cry!

3. Steve could be a <u>mystery shopper</u>. He says, "Shop till you drop!"

4. I wonder if a <u>perfume tester</u> needs strong skin or sensitive skin.

5. A <u>dog walker</u> has to be careful that the dog doesn't get away.

6. A <u>zookeeper</u> has to get used to strong smells.

7. Every movie production has a <u>best boy</u>.

8. I'd be afraid to be a <u>lion tamer</u>. It seems like a very dangerous job!

B. Listen to the sentences to check your predictions.

C. Work with a partner and take turns reading the sentences.

A. Work with a partner. Write **A**, **P**, or **C** next to each expression in the speech bubbles according to whether it's used to:

- ask for clarification (A).
- paraphrase someone's idea (P).
- clarify an idea (C).

B. Choose a job mentioned in this unit. Give your opinion about the job and discuss it with your partner. Use the language from Part A.

PRACTICE 10

A. On the lines below, rewrite these disorganized paragraphs making any necessary revisions.

1. Speleologists are usually university-trained scientists who have studied geology, biology, chemistry, hydrology, and climatology, but some speleologists are self-trained. A speleologist, someone who explores caves for a living, loves delving into cramped, dark caves. Just think of all the wonderful and strange things you can find in a cave.

_____

_____

_____

_____

_____

_____

_____

_____

_____

_____

2. Examples of dangerous jobs are truck driver, taxi driver, airplane pilot, security guard, construction worker, and farm worker. Some people like to do these kinds of jobs even though they know they are at a higher risk of injury. Would you like to do these jobs?

_____

_____

_____

_____

_____

_____

_____

_____

_____

_____

B. Discuss your revisions with a partner.

YOU'RE IN CHARGE!

UNIT FIVE OBJECTIVES: How well did you meet the objectives for this unit? Check the box next to each objective you feel you mastered.

GRAMMAR	LISTENING	SPEAKING
The passive voice	❏ Recognizing categories	Maintaining understanding in a discussion
❏ Use in present tense		❏ Asking for clarification
❏ Use in past tense		❏ Clarifying an idea
❏ Use with modal verbs		❏ Paraphrasing an idea

PRONUNCIATION	READING	WRITING
❏ Stress patterns in compound nouns and adjectives	❏ Making graphic organizers	❏ Writing an introduction

LEARNING STRATEGIES: Reflect on your use of learning strategies and thinking skills in this unit. What are some of the strategies you employed? Which ones were most successful for you?

Write your thoughts here.

_____

_____

_____

_____

_____

_____

_____

_____

_____

Unit 5 Learning Strategies
• Making inferences
• Categorizing
• Using prior knowledge
• Using graphic organizers
• Using context to determine meaning
• Noting main ideas
• Noting details
• Brainstorming
• Comparing
• Working cooperatively

PRACTICE 1

Work with a partner. Give an explanation and a real-life example of each proverb and share it with the class.

PROVERBS

- A smile will gain you ten more years of life.
- The eyes are the mirror of the soul.
- Handsome is as handsome does.

PRACTICE 2

Complete the crossword puzzle. Refer to page 68 in your student book for help.

ACROSS

3. egg-shaped
5. reddish brown
7. decide on, choose
9. short and heavily built
11. in the shape of a heart
13. well-defined muscles, no fat

DOWN

1. hair on a man's chin or jaw
2. facial hair above lips
4. cut very short
6. pale or yellow hair
8. hair on chin only
10. looking like waves
12. greenish brown

A. Two friends are discussing changes they would like to make in their appearance. Work with a partner. Complete the conversation.

ROLES	CONVERSATION	FUNCTIONS
Martin:	If you could change something about your appearance, what would you change?	Ask a hypothetical question.
Iris:	I think I'd change _____, as long as it made me look better.	Give information and set a condition.
Martin:	I'd want to see a computer image first, just in case _____.	Remark on the condition.
Iris:	That's a good idea.	Reply to the response.

B. Take turns being the two friends and use the cues to talk about other possible changes.

    a. hair style   **b.** hair type   **c.** body type   **d.** eyeglasses

PRACTICE 4

Complete the conversation with the appropriate form of the verbs in parentheses.

TYRONE: If you **(1. change)** _____ anything about your hair, what **(2. you / change)** _____?

RUTH: Well, I think I **(3. make)** _____ it straight instead of curly. If I **(4. have)** _____ straight hair, I **(5. not/need to)** _____ use hair gel on it every morning!

TYRONE: H-m-m-m-m, but if you **(6. want)** _____ to have straight hair, first you **(7. need to)** _____ let it grow longer. Then you **(8. have to)** _____ get it straightened by a hair stylist. If you **(9. decide to)** _____ do it, I **(10. take)** _____ you to a good place I know. But if you **(11. get)** _____ it straightened, **(12. you / want to)** _____ _____ keep it the same color or change that too?

RUTH: Whew! I don't know. That's a good question. I'm not sure I **(13. like)** _____ to change the color. If I **(14. do)** _____that, maybe it **(15. be)** _____ too much. If I **(16. decide)** _____ to have straight hair, I **(17. see)** _____ how I like it first, then I **(18. consider)** _____ what else I might do.

PRACTICE 5

Work with a partner. Use the cues to ask and answer questions using third conditional.

Example:

Q: What would **Julie's parents** have done if **Julie had dyed her hair purple**?

A: If **Julie had dyed her hair purple**, her parents would have grounded her.

> **Cues**
>
> a. Julie's parents / Julie dye hair purple
>
> b. Your father / mother take a modeling course
>
> c. Your best friend / you cut your hair
>
> d. You / your sister get her teeth fixed
>
> e. You / your best friend gain weight
>
> f. Phillip / his father shave his head
>
> g. (your own idea)

PRACTICE 6

Look at the pictures and decide what these people are thinking. Write sentences underneath the pictures using first, second, or third conditionals. Share your sentences with a partner.

a. <u>If I grow tall, I'll be a basketball</u>
<u>player.</u>

b. _____

_____

(continued on next page)

c. _____

_____

d. _____

_____

e. _____

_____

f. _____

_____

PRACTICE 7

Complete the sentences using *in case* or *as long as* and your own ideas. In some cases, either expression is possible. Share your answers with a partner.

1. I think I'll use a temporary hair color for now _____.

2. I'll throw away my glasses _____.

3. She didn't tell her husband about the cosmetic surgery _____.

4. He took a baseball cap to the hair stylist's _____.

5. _____, I've decided to buy some new clothes.

6. I'm going to ask the dentist to give me an anesthetic _____.

7. _____, she's just getting one ear pierced at a time.

8. My brother is working out at the gym _____.

PRACTICE 8

Work with a partner. Look at the situations. Use *only if*, *as long as*, and *in case* to talk about the possibilities.

Situation need eyeglasses

Example: Partner: When are you getting your eyeglasses?

You: As long as I need to see better, I'm thinking of getting contact lenses.

> **Situations**
> need teeth fixed
> going bald
> need to lose weight
> need to gain weight
> need to get more sleep
> (your own idea)

PRACTICE 9

A. **Before You Listen** Discuss with a partner. Who was considered a great beauty in the legend and history of your culture? Who is considered a great beauty in your culture today? What role have these people played in your culture?

B. Listen to a panel discussion on figures in history and legend known for their beauty and take notes to complete the chart. When you have finished, compare your notes with your partner's.

Helen of Troy

Main Ideas	Notes
Name of the legendary figure discussed	
Major historical event with which she is associated	
Parents according to legend	
Husband chosen for her	
Person she ran away with	
Two contrasting views of the woman's character	

PRACTICE 10

A. Predict the intonation pattern of the italicized words in the conversations. Mark the words with ↘ or ↗ to show the intonation you think the speakers will use.

1. A: Mom! *Surprise*! I got a new hairstyle.

　　B: Oh *fantastic*!

　　A: No, *really*! It's *awesome*

　　B: *Yeah, right.*

2. A: Look at *that*! Margot got her head shaved!

　　B: *What*?

　　A: Yeah, *look*!

　　B: *Awful*!

3. A: I saw Roseanne at the mall.

　　B: *And*?

　　A: She's lost sixty pounds.

　　B: *No*!

　　A: Exercise and dieting.

　　B: That's *amazing*!

　　A: *Yeah*!

B. Listen to the conversations to check your predictions.

C. Work with a partner and take turns reading the conversations.

PRACTICE 11

Work in groups of three. Choose a topic from the list. Take turns discussing the topic according to the roles given. After you finish, change roles and discuss another topic.

PERSON A: Say something about the topic.
　　　　　　　Elaborate on the topic.

PERSON B: Digress from the topic.

PERSON C: Bring the discussion back on track politely.

> **Topics**
> - Beauty in Nature
> - Helen of Troy and other Historical Beauties
> - The Latest Styles and Trends
> - Improving Your Appearance

Finish the introduction to this essay with your own ideas. Then write three supporting paragraphs that discuss and support your ideas.

Beauty Is in the Eye of the Beholder

    The concept of beauty has certainly changed through the ages. It also varies from culture to culture. So what exactly is beauty? In my mind, beauty

YOU'RE IN CHARGE!

UNIT SIX OBJECTIVES: How well did you meet the objectives for this unit? Check the box next to each objective you feel you mastered.

GRAMMAR	LISTENING	SPEAKING
❏ First, second, and third conditionals ❏ Adverbial expressions with the conditional	❏ Recognizing cause and effect relationships	❏ Keeping a conversation on track

PRONUNCIATION	READING	WRITING
❏ Rising and falling intonation to convey meaning	❏ Evaluating supporting examples	❏ Writing support paragraphs

LEARNING STRATEGIES: Reflect on your use of learning strategies and thinking skills in this unit. What are some of the strategies you employed? Which ones were most successful for you?

Write your thoughts here.

_____

_____

_____

_____

_____

_____

_____

_____

_____

_____

Unit 6 Learning Strategies
- Making inferences
- Categorizing
- Using prior knowledge
- Using context to determine meaning
- Noting main ideas
- Noting details
- Brainstorming
- Looking for cause/effect relationships
- Working cooperatively
- Analyzing

PRACTICE 1

Imagine that you live in a world where most people are left-handed. Work with a partner. Brainstorm five ways that world would be different from this one. Share your ideas with the class.

PRACTICE 2

Use the words in the box to complete the sentences.

| bias |
| derive |
| embedded |
| dread |
| exemplary |
| rejected |
| reveal |
| synonymous |

1. Studies _____ that right-hand dominance is located mostly in the left hemisphere of the brain and vice versa.

2. Some left-handed people feel that there is a definite _____ in favor of right-handed people.

3. An Internet web site selling products for left-handers is _____ of how life has improved for left-handers.

4. Negative attitudes about the left are still _____ in our everyday language.

5. Nabil _____ the pair of sneakers the salesperson brought because the right sneaker felt too tight.

6. The use of left is _____ with the lack of physical coordination, as in *two left feet*.

7. Many attitudes about the word *left* _____ from myths and superstitions.

8. As a left-handed person, I _____ using a right-hand pair of scissors.

PRACTICE 3

A. A right-handed student and a left-handed student are discussing the advantages of being left-handed. Work with a partner. Complete the conversation.

ROLES	CONVERSATION	FUNCTIONS
Right-handed person:	Are there advantages to being left-handed?	Ask a question.
Left-handed person:	Yes! A person who is left-handed _____ _____	Answer the question and give details.
Right-handed person:	Do you mean that a person who is left-handed _____ _____?	Ask a follow-up question.
Left-handed person:	Yes, a person who is left-handed can _____ _____	Answer the question and elaborate.

B. Take turns being the right-handed and left-handed students and use the cues below.

    a. advantages of being right-handed

    b. disadvantages of being left-handed

    c. disadvantages of being right-handed

PRACTICE 4

A. Write **D** if the italicized clause is defining and **ND** if it is nondefining. Add commas as necessary.

    _____ **1.** Scientists *who have studied handedness* say that seventy to ninety-five percent of the world's population is predominately right-handed.

    _____ **2.** Right-handed people *who are the majority* often don't realize how left-handers' needs are ignored.

    _____ **3.** Parents *who are both left-handed* can still have a right-handed child.

    _____ **4.** That book *which came on the market last year* teaches your left-handed child to write.

    _____ **5.** Most of the left-handers *whom Dr. Links interviewed* said that they used their right hand for a lot of things.

    _____ **6.** Roberto's sister *who is left-handed* is an excellent tennis player.

B. Work with a partner. Compare your answers and explain your choices.

PRACTICE 5

Read each numbered sentence and check the statement that best describes it.

1. A left-hand computer mouse, which is about as cheap as a right-hand one, can make the computer easier for left-handers to use.
   - ☐ Only a cheaper left-hand mouse makes the computer easier to use.
   - ☐ A left-hand mouse makes it easier for a left-hander to use the computer.

2. Piano players who are left-handed often find it easier to play the bass clef parts.
   - ☐ All piano players find it easier to play bass clef parts.
   - ☐ Left-handed piano players often find it easier to play bass clef parts.

3. Left-handers, who are often forgotten by product makers, have learned to adapt despite inconveniences.
   - ☐ Left-handers have adapted to inconveniences despite being forgotten by product makers.
   - ☐ Some left-handers are forgotten by product makers while others are remembered.

4. My friends who are right-handed usually forget to put me at the left end of the table when they invite me for dinner.
   - ☐ All my friends are right-handed, so they all forget to put me at the left end of the table.
   - ☐ Only my right-handed friends forget to put me at the left end of the table.

PRACTICE 6

A. Complete the sentences with appropriate relative pronouns.

1. Stewardesses is the longest English word _____ we can type with only the left hand.

2. Some famous people _____ have held powerful positions have been left-handed.

3. A left-hander _____ computer mouse has been specially adjusted can use the mouse more easily.

4. The girl _____ I was sitting next to in class was using a left-handed desk.

5. Approximately sixty percent of the people _____ are left-handed have speech controlled by the left hemisphere of the brain, like right-handers.

6. Looking at a baby _____ was just born, can you tell what handedness the child will have?

B. Work with a partner. Compare your answers and explain your choices.

Combine the pairs of sentences using *whose* and rewrite them on the lines.
Use the second sentence as an adjective clause. Make any necessary changes.

Example: Stephen's son is left-handed.   His name is Alex.

Stephen's son, whose name is Alex, is left-handed.

1. Ken uses the new desk every day.   His desk is a left hand one.

_____

2. Mary is left-handed.   Her car is specially equipped.

_____

3. That man lent his pen to me.   We interviewed his wife.

_____

4. Tomoko is a talented artist.   Her pictures are beautiful.

_____

5. That company is very small.   I bought their left-hand scissors.

_____

6. Ms. Chekov won a big teaching award.   Her students are all left-handed.

_____

PRACTICE 8

Complete these sentences. Then share them with the class.

1. Yesterday, I met a boy whose _____ makes
left-hand furniture.

2. The woman whom _____ told us it was on the next corner.

3. Steffie, who _____, won the chess championship.

4. The soccer ball that _____ was signed by Ronaldo.

5. That computer mouse, which _____, was made
for left-handers.

6. A left-hand desk is one that _____.

PRACTICE 9

A. **Before You Listen** Discuss with a partner. What's your favorite store to shop in? What do they sell? What do you like to buy there?

B. Listen to a telephone conversation where someone is asking for information. Check the statement that summarizes the main idea of the conversation.

_____ Two people are talking about buying left-hand products on the Internet.

_____ Two people are talking about the store being in existence for seven years.

_____ Two people are talking about the store having a web page and a catalogue.

_____ Two people are talking about products for left-handed children that are available in the store.

_____ Two people are talking about the Westside Mall.

C. Listen again and decide if the statements are **T** (true) or **F** (false). Compare your answers with a partner's.

_____ **1.** The telephone caller already knows that the store has been in existence for seven years.

_____ **2.** The caller's husband is left-handed.

_____ **3.** The caller heard about the store from her friend.

_____ **4.** The sales clerk offers to mail a catalogue to the caller.

_____ **5.** The sales clerk mentions a handwriting series and a reading series.

_____ **6.** The caller's husband plays the guitar.

_____ **7.** The caller talks about visiting the store next week.

_____ **8.** The store is located on the third floor of the Westside Mall.

PRACTICE 10

A. Predict which sounds in the boldfaced words will be affected by a neighboring sound. Underline the affected parts of the words.

> **Example:** We'*re in* the money.

1. They went to visit **Land's End**.
2. **She's socially** acquainted with them.
3. **He's serious**.
4. That's the store where we **went to** find gloves.
5. She wore a **black cape**.
6. I **washed** all the dishes.
7. **Let's eat** some **asparagus soup**.
8. They **cooked** a wonderful dinner.

B. Listen to the sentences to check your predictions.

C. Work with a partner and take turns reading the sentences.

PRACTICE 11

A. Decide if these expressions are **E** (encouraging elaboration) or **P** (encouraging participation).

_____ 1. What's your perspective on this, Mari?

_____ 2. What are the deeper implications of this proposal?

_____ 3. You're being very quiet over there, Ruslan. Tell us what <u>you</u> think.

_____ 4. Mr. Kim usually sees another side. What do you say, Mr. Kim?

_____ 5. I still don't think we've gotten to the root of this. What's its real impact?

_____ 6. That's what we see on the surface. What's under the surface?

_____ 7. Let's try to take this a bit further.

_____ 8. Why don't we see what Susana thinks about this?

B. Work in small groups. Your company has decided to make its office more user-friendly for left-handers. Discuss changes you will need to make. Use expressions from Part A in your discussion.

A. Read the following essay and write a conclusion. Choose one of the techniques you practiced in the student book to write a concluding paragraph.

Tips for the Lefty

What do a three-ring binder, a guitar, and surgical instruments have in common? The answer is that they all present special challenges for left-handed people to use. Perhaps young left-handers can benefit from the experiences of older lefties with these tips in the area of school, music, and health.

To solve the problem of having to use three-ring loose-leaf binders in school, take the paper out of the binder and use the hard binder as an extension of your desk. Place the paper on top of the binder, making sure that the binder is slanted toward you, and it will be more comfortable. Another tip is to do more keyboarding and less handwriting. While you are at the computer keyboard, change your mouse preferences to left hand. That should drive everyone else crazy!

In the music world, left-hand guitars are more expensive than the commonly used right-hand ones. There are ways, however, for a lefty to adapt. You can play left-handed and learn the chords and fingerings upside down. There are special chord and scale books to help you with that. You can buy a cheap, old, right-hand guitar and convert it to a left-hand one by restringing and reversing the bridge. If all else fails, you can simply learn to play right-handed and use your stronger, more coordinated left hand for the chords and fingering.

Healthwise, if you are left-handed and studying to be a surgeon, be prepared to learn to use instruments with your right hand. Otherwise, the entire operating room may need to be rearranged. If you are ever hospitalized, make sure to tell the nurses to put the IV (intravenous) in your right arm so that you can write, draw, or hold a book comfortably. If you have frequent back pains, check what kind of desk you are using and your position when you write. A left-handed person using a right hand desk can develop back problems.

_____

_____

_____

_____

_____

B. Work in small groups. Share your conclusions and answer these questions.

- What concluding technique did you use?
- Are any features of your conclusion similar to the introduction?

YOU'RE IN CHARGE!

UNIT SEVEN OBJECTIVES: How well did you meet the objectives for this unit? Check the box next to each objective you feel you mastered.

GRAMMAR	LISTENING	SPEAKING
❑ Defining and nondefining adjective clauses ❑ Adjective clauses with *whose*	❑ Listening to summarize the key ideas	Keeping a discussion going ❑ Encouraging more thorough treatment ❑ Encouraging more participation

PRONUNCIATION	READING	WRITING
❑ Sounds affected by the presence of a neighboring sound	❑ Identifying generalizations ❑ Identifying qualifying statements	Analytical essays ❑ Writing a concluding paragraph

LEARNING STRATEGIES: Reflect on your use of learning strategies and thinking skills in this unit. What are some of the strategies you employed? Which ones were most successful for you?

Write your thoughts here.

_____

_____

_____

_____

_____

_____

_____

_____

_____

Unit 7 Learning Strategies
• Categorizing
• Using prior knowledge
• Using context to determine meaning
• Noting details
• Brainstorming
• Summarizing key ideas
• Working cooperatively

PRACTICE 1

Personality can be defined as the sum of a person's behavioral and emotional characteristics. Work in small groups to discuss these questions.

- Do you think that personality is unchangeable, or can it be reshaped?

- If it were possible to reshape your personality, would you change it? In what ways?

PRACTICE 2

Use the words in the box to complete the sentences.

1. Ari's music class _____ a show for the parents.

2. Carmen is a very reserved person. She tends to_____ when she meets new people.

3. Debbie gave Steve a new assignment that he is trying to _____.

4. Maya is very shy so it is hard for her to _____ at parties.

5. You should _____ your mind about what course you want to study.

6. Let's _____ that documentary on brain research.

> carry out
> hold back
> look at
> open up
> put on
> make up

PRACTICE 3

A. Two cousins, Fred and Manuel, are discussing their family. Work with a partner. Complete the conversation.

ROLES	CONVERSATION	FUNCTIONS
Fred:	Who in our family would you say is very outgoing and funny?	Ask about personality traits
Manuel:	Well, I'd say that _____ _____.	Give a brief description of your choice.
Fred:	Well, I'd agree about being outgoing, but not _____.	Respond and give an opinion.
Manuel:	Oh, really? Why do you say that?	Ask for an explanation.
Fred:	I think _____ _____.	Respond and give support to your opinion.

B. Take turns being the two cousins and use the cues to discuss other family members.

    a. sensible and passionate   **d.** reserved and analytical

    b. strong-willed and sociable   **e.** studious and ambitious

    c. hardworking and generous   **f.** (your own idea)

PRACTICE 4

Circle the letter of the expression that best fits each sentence.

1. Eleanor went to the library to _____ information on Barcelona.

    a. look in   **b.** look up   **c.** look out

2. Martin's very sick with the flu. I hope he _____ it soon!

    a. gets off   **b.** gets on   **c.** gets over

3. Jake loves a challenge. He _____ people who are complicated and difficult.

    a. goes for   **b.** goes over   **c.** goes through

4. Elise will never finish her studies unless she _____ watching TV.

    a. gives over   **b.** gives into   **c.** gives up

5. Mari has decided to _____ starting her new diet until next Monday.

    a. put off   **b.** put on   **c.** put up

6. Mei-Li, your headset is very loud! The whole bus can hear it. Could you please _____ it _____?

    a. turn . . . up   **b.** turn . . . down   **c.** turn . . . over

PRACTICE 5

Work with a partner. Take turns describing what you see in the pictures using the phrasal verbs in the box.

point out	back up	look up to	run into
back out	call up	go over	put on
call on	turn down	turn off	

1.

2.

3.

4.

My teacher is the greatest!

5.

And this will be your bedroom with the skylight that you can open.

6.

PRACTICE 6

Complete the sentences with the correct particle from the box.

back	into	off	on
out	over	up	

1. To go from here to the museum, you need to get _____ the bus and ride it to the corner of State and Main. It's the seventh stop.

2. When Omar got _____ the car, he forgot to fasten his seatbelt, and the police stopped him.

3. Pablo got _____ the bus in front of the theater and walked to the corner coffee shop.

4. What time do you usually get _____ in the morning?

5. Lili got _____ the chickenpox just in time to be in her school play.

6. First David paid the driver; then he got _____ of the taxi.

7. When did José get _____ last night? It must have been very late.

PRACTICE 7

A. Match the phrases on the left with those on the right to make logical sentences.

1. This noise is driving me crazy
2. It's so hot in this room
3. Silvia is so busy
4. Cindy is very involved in environmental issues
5. Mark is easygoing
6. Liza isn't easy for some people to understand at first
7. Hisako starts studying at the university next year
8. Marcia and Tom are very compatible

a. and usually *goes along with* what his friends want to do.

b. and she *comes across as* distant.

c. and she's really *looking forward to* it.

d. so they *get along* well when they do joint projects.

e. and *looks down on* people who waste and litter.

f. but I guess we'll just have to *put up* with it.

g. that she should *take off* her heavy coat.

h. because she *puts off* her responsibilities until the last minute.

B. Work with a partner. Compare your answers and take turns reading the completed sentences.

PRACTICE 8

Work with a partner. Write the phrasal verbs in parentheses in the correct order on the blank lines.

Example: Freddie has new job responsibilities. I hope he'll be able

to ____carry them out____.
        (them / carry out)

1. Melissa and Roberto have just had their baby. Let's go to the hospital

 and _____.
     (them / check up on)

2. For a moment I couldn't remember where I had met you, but then

 suddenly it _____.
     (came to / me)

3. We still don't have the solution to the puzzle. But don't worry—

 we'll _____.
     (it / figure out)

4. I tried to keep Marcia from jumping into the freezing lake, but

 I couldn't _____.
     (her / hold back)

5. Toby hoped to get that part in the play, but the director _____.
         (him / turned down)

6. You got the letter! What are you waiting for? _____!
         (it / Open up)

7. I don't know how much it'll cost to fly there, but I'll _____.
         (it / look into)

PRACTICE 9

Complete the sentences with your own ideas. Then share them with the class.

1. I've always looked up to _____.

2. Professor Chin just got over _____.

3. They turned down _____.

4. We put off the concert _____.

5. Our personalities are made up of _____.

6. I just figured out your _____.

PRACTICE 10

A.   Before You Listen Discuss with a partner. What are the different personality theories you've learned about? Which one do you find the most interesting? Which one do you think is the most accurate?

B.   Listen to a group of people giving their opinions. Decide if the sentences are **T** (true) or **F** (false).

_____ **1.** The people are talking about the order in which they were born in their own families.

_____ **2.** Type A and Type B are similar personality types.

_____ **3.** Astrology is another personality theory.

_____ **4.** Birth order theory has to do with whether you graduated first from high school.

_____ **5.** According to the discussion, color preference determines your hair color.

C.   Listen to the conversation again and fill in the chart.

Person	Favorite Personality Theory	Reason
Margaret		
William		
Elizabeth		
Elton		

D.   Compare your answers with a partner's and explain your choices.

E.   Discuss in small groups. Which of the speakers did you agree with? In your opinion, which speaker had the best reason for his or her choice?

PRACTICE 11

A. Predict the stress patterns of the two-and three-verb combinations in italics. Underline the stressed words.

1. Ambitious people *look for* ways to advance.

2. People who are reserved hesitate to *ask for* things.

3. Bosses often like to *check up on* their employees.

4. He had an appointment, so he had to *turn down* Jeremy's invitation.

5. We might *run into* some bad weather today.

6. I'm *looking forward to* meeting your partner.

7. Let's *turn on* the news and *find out* what happened.

8. She had to *give up* tennis because of her bad knee.

B. Listen to the sentences to check your predictions.

C. Work with a partner and take turns reading the sentences.

PRACTICE 12

You are taking part in a panel discussion on whether astrology is a science or entertainment. Work in groups of three. Take turns playing the roles in the box. Use expressions for turn taking and giving up the floor in your discussion.

Roles

Rosa: You are the group leader. You need to make sure that everyone participates.

Larry: You are easygoing and afraid to impose your opinions.

Misha: You are very outspoken and like to dominate a conversation.

PRACTICE 13

Write an essay comparing two personality theories. First decide which three aspects you are going to compare in your point-by-point support paragraphs. Fill in the following outline before writing.

COMPARING:

_____ personality theory with _____ personality theory

POINT 1: _____

POINT 2: _____

POINT 3: _____

YOU'RE IN CHARGE!

UNIT EIGHT OBJECTIVES: How well did you meet the objectives for this unit?
Check the box next to each objective you feel you mastered.

GRAMMAR

Phrasal verbs
- ❏ Separable
- ❏ Inseparable

LISTENING

- ❏ Listening to relate information to one's own life

SPEAKING

Having the floor in a discussion
- ❏ Taking turns
- ❏ Giving up the floor
- ❏ Refusing to give up the floor

PRONUNCIATION

- ❏ Stress patterns in two- and three-word verb combinations

READING

- ❏ Making inferences from the reading

WRITING

- ❏ Analyzing a point-by-point essay for comparison or contrast

LEARNING STRATEGIES: Reflect on your use of learning strategies and thinking skills in this unit. What are some of the strategies you employed? Which ones were most successful for you?

Write your thoughts here.

_____

_____

_____

_____

_____

_____

_____

_____

_____

_____

Unit 8 Learning Strategies
- Using prior knowledge
- Using context to determine meaning
- Analyzing differences
- Making predictions
- Categorizing
- Comparing and contrasting
- Working cooperatively
- Making inferences
- Brainstorming

PRACTICE 1

Work with a partner. Draw an imaginary gadget that represents a new advance in technology. Decide on its purpose, function, and purchase price. Present your ideas and drawing to the class.

PRACTICE 2

Match the definitions from the box with the italicized words in the sentences.

> **a.** a plastic or metal card worn to show employment in an organization
> **b.** without permission
> **c.** a secret copy of a message
> **d.** relating to principles of what is right or wrong
> **e.** illegal copying to sell or use

_____ **1.** Software *piracy* is a big problem for the information technology industry.

_____ **2.** High-level officials of governments are having discussions about what constitutes *ethical* behavior.

_____ **3.** With the sophisticated equipment that exists today, unethical people can make *unauthorized* copies of video games, music, and software programs.

_____ **4.** Some technology companies make employees wear special *badges* or carry security cards to enter their buildings.

_____ **5.** Mr. Fonseca always sends a *blind copy* to his boss of his important emails.

PRACTICE 3

A. Marco and Li-Ding are friends. They are looking at a cell phone that Marco just bought. Work with a partner. Complete the conversation.

ROLES	CONVERSATION	FUNCTIONS
Marco:	I need help with my cell phone.	State a need.
Li-Ding:	All right. _____ _____ _____ ?	Respond and ask for specifics.
Marco:	I want to learn how to make a call. _____ _____ _____ .	Specify, adding more information.
Li-Ding:	Fine. Well, first you _____ _____ _____ .	Explain and generalize.

B. Take turns being Marco and Li-Ding and discuss other cell phone functions.

a. how to receive a call   **c.** how to store telephone numbers

b. how to listen to a message   **d.** how to recharge the battery

PRACTICE 4

Work with a partner. Read the following conversation. Then create similar conversations using the cues in the box. Take turns with the roles.

KEN: I want to buy **a new printer**.

LUCIA: Oh, really? Do you want **a laser printer** or **an ink-jet one**?

KEN: I'm afraid **the printer** will have to be **an ink-jet one**. **A laser printer** is too expensive.

LUCIA: Wait! The one I saw yesterday was on sale and almost as cheap as **an ink-jet printer**.

KEN: Can you take me to the store? I want to see it!

> **a.** computer—laptop or desktop
> **b.** digital camera—large memory or small memory
> **c.** cell phone—e-mail/ phone combination or standard
> **d.** Internet access—high-speed DSL or phone line
> **e.** (your own idea)

PRACTICE 5

Read the following sentences and correct any errors in the use of articles. Then work with a partner to compare and explain your corrections.

1. I need to find ~~the~~ *a* computer shop. There must be one near here.
2. He went to the computer shop on a corner.
3. I'll go to the bank to get money to buy myself the computer.
4. Do you have the cell phone? I need to find one.
5. To open our garage you need to push a remote control above the rearview mirror.
6. Do you heat your house with the solar power, the gas, or electricity?
7. Let's watch a DVD video I gave you tonight. It's really good.
8. He has the pressure-sensitive floor in his house.

PRACTICE 6

A. Complete the sentences with appropriate articles. In some cases, no article is necessary.

Anya got **(1.)** _____ new computer last week, and she has been on it as much as possible ever since. She has sent **(2.)** _____ e-mail messages and has spent a lot of time on **(3.)** _____ Internet. **(4.)** _____ Internet has opened up **(5.)** _____ whole new world for her!

(6.) _____ other day, Anya discovered **(7.)** _____ *National Geographic* web site and stayed on it for hours. She "visited" **(8.)** _____ Yellowstone Park, then jumped over to **(9.)** _____ Lake Victoria, **(10.)** _____ second largest lake in **(11.)** _____ world, then went down **(12.)** _____ Nile River from Aswan to Cairo. Later she went to **(13.)** _____ United States and toured New York City along **(14.)** _____ 5th Avenue all the way up to **(15.)** _____ Central Park. Then she decided to go to **(16.)** _____ Europe, starting with **(17.)** _____ Netherlands, as **(18.)** _____ grandmother had come from there. Anya loved **(19.)** _____ canals in Amsterdam and **(20.)** _____ beautiful flowers everywhere.

After all that surfing, Anya was so tired, she had to take **(21.)** _____ nap. She woke up **(22.)** _____ hour later and went right back on **(23.)** _____ computer. She decided she would like to see **(24.)** _____ news, so she opened **(25.)** _____ browser and typed in **(26.)** _____ name of her favorite

(continued on next page)

newspaper. Right away, **(27.)** _____ news was on **(28.)** _____ screen. She quickly scanned **(29.)** _____ headlines and then decided to enter **(30.)** _____ name of her favorite sport: **(31.)** _____ soccer. When Anya did that, she got **(32.)** _____ huge choice of teams, statistics, stadiums, and famous players. She even found **(33.)** _____ forum where she could write comments or ask questions and get responses from other fans. She found **(34.)** _____ chatroom site where she could talk online about her favorite team to **(35.)** _____ other people.

  (36.) _____ computer definitely had her fascinated. She hoped her fascination wouldn't become **(37.)** _____ computer addiction!

B.   Work with a partner. Compare your answers and explain your choices.

PRACTICE 7

A.   Before You Listen Discuss with a partner. What influences your decision to buy or not to buy something? What electronic products, if any, have you bought in the last year?

B.   Listen to two commercials. What are they advertising? Work with a partner and summarize the main idea of each advertisement.

SUMMARY OF ADVERTISEMENT 1:

_____

SUMMARY OF ADVERTISEMENT 2:

_____

C. Listen again and fill in the charts with the information you might use to decide if you will buy these products.

ADVERTISEMENT 1

Product	
Features	
Name	
Price	
Where sold	

ADVERTISEMENT 2

Product	
Features	
Name	
Price	
Where sold	

PRACTICE 8

A. Predict which words in the conversations should receive confirming stress and underline them.

1. A: Did you say DVDs can hold up to 85 megabytes of data?

   B: No, 8.5 gigabytes.

2. A: Was that four hours of movies on a DVD?

   B: Yes, four.

3. A: DVDs come in two formats: DVD-Video and DVD-ROM.

   B: Did you say DVD-RAM?

   A: No, ROM!

4. A: The laser printer is based on technology used by photographers, right?

   B: No, not photographers, photocopiers!

   A: Oh, photocopiers!

5. A: So the optical scanner is a computer output device?

   B: No, it's an input device.

B. Listen to the conversations to check your predictions.

C. Work with a partner and take turns reading the conversations.

A. Decide if the following sentences represent **B** (blocking behavior) or **M** (managing blocking behavior).

_____ **1.** This is off the subject, but don't you think the company could provide some coffee and snacks for us during these long meetings?

_____ **2.** I'll go along with anything, as long as you don't change my vacation plans. I told you about that cruise, didn't I?

_____ **3.** Bing, I think you and Lisa can work out where we're going to eat at another time. We really need to stick to the agenda right now.

_____ **4.** By the way, did you see the report about that private school on the news last night? Isn't that shocking?

_____ **5.** I think that point was settled earlier in the meeting. We'll gain nothing by rediscussing it now. Let's move on.

_____ **6.** Tom, we can't hold up the meeting for you to find the memo. Let's get back to that later.

B. You are on a special technology committee at your school. Your responsibility is to give recommendations on new computer equipment for the school.

Work in groups of three. Discuss ideas with your committee members, take turns trying to block the discussion or manage the blocking behavior. Use the expressions in Part A in your discussion.

PRACTICE 10

A. Brainstorm three similarities between e-mail communication and telephone communication. List your three points here.

POINT 1: _____

                   (a) e-mail communication
                   (b) telephone communication

POINT 2: _____

                   (a) e-mail communication
                   (b) telephone communication

POINT 3: _____

                   (a) e-mail communication
                   (b) telephone communication

B. Write a point-by-point essay of comparison. Remember to include an introduction and a conclusion. Begin your introduction below.

_____

_____

_____

_____

_____

_____

_____

_____

C. Exchange papers with a partner. Use the questions in the box to give feedback to your partner. Make any necessary revisions to your essay.

- Is there a clear introduction with a thesis statement?
- Are the supporting paragraphs organized in a clear, point-by-point sequence?
- Have transition words been used appropriately?
- Is there a clear conclusion?

YOU'RE IN CHARGE!

UNIT NINE OBJECTIVES: How well did you meet the objectives for this unit? Check the box next to each objective you feel you mastered.

GRAMMAR
- ❑ Definite article
- ❑ Indefinite articles

LISTENING
- ❑ Listening to identify implications

SPEAKING
Managing disruptive behavior in a discussion
- ❑ Blocking behavior
- ❑ Managing blocking behavior

PRONUNCIATION
- ❑ Using confirming stress for clarification

READING
- ❑ Assessing the function(s) of a text

WRITING
- ❑ Writing a point-by-point comparative essay
- ❑ Using transition words to show similarities

LEARNING STRATEGIES: Reflect on your use of learning strategies and thinking skills in this unit. What are some of the strategies you employed? Which ones were most successful for you?

Write your thoughts here.

_____

_____

_____

_____

_____

_____

_____

_____

_____

_____

_____

Unit 9 Learning Strategies
- Using prior knowledge
- Using context to determine meaning
- Analyzing similarities
- Making predictions
- Categorizing
- Summarizing
- Noting details
- Comparing and contrasting
- Working cooperatively
- Making inferences
- Brainstorming

Many people believe that we are not alone in the universe. Privately funded organizations are searching for extraterrestrial life using expensive radio and optical telescope equipment. Discuss with a partner.

- Do you believe that there is life in other places in the universe? Explain.

- Is it worthwhile to spend money on projects to locate extraterrestrial life? State your reasons.

SETI radio telescope

PRACTICE 2

Use the words in the box to complete the sentences.

commonplace	grueling	seasoned	shrink
deteriorate	prominent	second thoughts	would-be

1. Several _____ donors are helping to fund the construction of radio telescopes to search for signals from outer space.

2. Due to the effects of gravity, astronauts' legs _____ during long periods spent in space.

3. Another effect of long-term stays in space is loss of muscle tone, causing the muscle tissue to _____.

4. The little _____ astronauts thoroughly enjoyed their stay at the NASA summer camp for children.

5. John is having _____ about his university major; he is now considering a change to astrophysics.

6. In the distant future, travel to other planets will be _____ and nothing out of the ordinary.

7. A _____ pilot is much less likely to panic in an emergency.

8. The mental and physical training astronauts must go through is often a _____ experience.

A. Two futurist experts are discussing their predictions at a university conference. Work with a partner. Complete the conversation.

ROLES	CONVERSATION	FUNCTIONS
Panelist 1:	I think by the year 2025, we'll be growing crops in space.	State a prediction about a specific time in space.
Panelist 2:	Oh really? That soon?	Express surprise.
Panelist 1:	Yes, by that time we will have developed _____ _____ .	Add more information about what would have been achieved by that time.
Panelist 2:	That's amazing! _____ _____ .	Respond and make a generalization.

B. Take turns being the experts and use the cues to discuss other predictions.

    a. raise animals in space

    b. achieve time travel

    c. prove the origin of the universe

    d. discover life on Mars

    e. find a tenth planet

    f. (your own idea)

PRACTICE 4

Some business leaders are discussing possibilities for future business development in space. Complete the sentences with appropriate forms of the verbs in parentheses.

MR. LONG: And so we all agree how important the development of commercial interests **(1. be)** _____ in the coming decades.

MR. KING: Yes, but I wonder when we **(2. begin)** _____ to see any profits from the enormous expenditures we **(3. make)** _____ in the first few years.

MS. HAHN: I'm sure that we **(4. have)** _____ to wait for a while, but I feel confident that we **(5. get)** _____ good returns on our investments by the year 2030.

MR. KING: How can you be so sure our investments **(6. make)** _____ a profit by then? It **(7. take)** _____ years for the general public to accept the idea of living away from Earth.

MS. HAHN: Oh, I agree with you there, but I'm talking about earthbound uses for the products we **(8. develop)** _____ for living in space.

MR. LONG: She's right. I **(9. give)** _____ you an example. We already use products originally developed for space in our daily lives, such as nitinol. It's a metal alloy we use in braces to straighten teeth.

MR. KING: OK, OK. I get it. The money I **(10. invest)** _____ over the next twenty years will eventually make its way back into my pocket!

PRACTICE 5

How do you envision the year 2050? Write sentences using the future progressive about what we will be doing and seeing. Then share your predictions with the class.

Example: We'll be using jet-propelled backpacks instead of driving cars.

1. _____.
2. _____.
3. _____.
4. _____.
5. _____.

PRACTICE 6

Read each numbered sentence and check the statement that best describes it.

1. Some people believe scientists will have discovered Planet X within the next two decades.

   ☐ It will take no more than twenty years to discover Planet X.

   ☐ Planet X was discovered after twenty years had passed.

2. By the 22nd century, we still won't have learned the secret of time travel.

   ☐ Time travel will not be achieved before the 22nd century.

   ☐ After the 22nd century we will not understand time travel.

3. Halley's comet will have been sighted again by the year 2061.

   ☐ Halley's comet will be seen again after 2061.

   ☐ People will next see Halley's comet before 2061.

4. By the end of this decade, scientists will have perfected a spaceship to withstand the heat of Venus.

   ☐ A spaceship that high temperatures on Venus won't destroy will be ready in about ten years.

   ☐ A spaceship that can withstand the heat of Venus was perfected a decade ago.

5. Some people believe SETI radio telescopes will have detected a signal within this century proving that extraterrestrial intelligence exists.

   ☐ A signal from extraterrestrial intelligence was detected at the end of the century.

   ☐ Before this century ends, there will be proof of the existence of extraterrestrial intelligence.

PRACTICE 7

A. Complete the sentences using the future perfect form of the verbs in parentheses.

1. By the end of this year, engineers (design) _____ a sealed whole-body shower for astronauts in space.

2. By the end of this year, Japanese scientists (experiment) _____ with reproducing and growing fresh fish for sushi in space.

3. By the end of this decade, more than 500 new satellites
   (replace) _____ an equal number of obsolete satellites.

4. By the end of this year, a cola drink company **(provide)** _____
   astronauts with special cans of cola that can be used in gravity-free environments.

5. Within this decade, scientists **(prove)** _____, experimentally, that a
   person can survive on the oxygen produced by plants in a sealed environment.

B. Work with a partner. Decide which of the statements in part A will come true.

PRACTICE 8

What will you have accomplished in your life ten years from now? Write sentences
using the future perfect. Share your sentences with the class.

> **Example:** <u>Within ten years, I will have learned to speak English fluently.</u>

1. _____.
2. _____.
3. _____.
4. _____.
5. _____.
6. _____.

PRACTICE 9

A. Before You Listen Discuss in small groups. If you could travel in space, what
planets, stars, and galaxies would you visit?

B. Listen to a radio show on space-related topics. Then answer the questions.

1. What causes black holes? _____
   _____.

2. What is escape velocity? _____
   _____.

3. What is the escape velocity of the Earth? _____
   _____.

4. Can anything escape from a black hole? _____
   _____.

5. What is known about white holes? _____
   _____.

C. Compare your answers with a partner's. How similar is your information?

A. Predict the rising-falling intonation patterns of the following sentences. Use arrows to mark the rise and fall of the pattern where new information begins.

Example: Another interesting theoretical concept is that of wormholes.

1. A combination of a black hole and a white hole is called a wormhole.

2. In theory, a black hole and a white hole could be separated by vast distances.

3. A white hole could even be in a different region of space time.

4. Entering a black hole and exiting a white hole would essentially result in time travel.

5. Theoretically, wormholes could connect two or more universes.

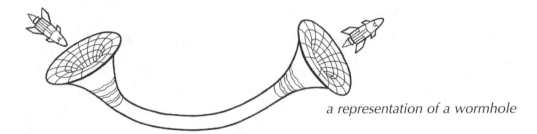

a representation of a wormhole

B. Listen to the sentences to check your predictions.

C. Work with a partner and take turns reading the sentences.

PRACTICE 11

You are a member of a special committee to evaluate new proposals for NASA projects. Work in small groups. Take turns discussing the proposals on the list. As you express your opinions, support your ideas by citing information from the sources listed in the box.

NEW PROPOSALS

- a proposal to study the effects on a mother and child of a year-long stay in space

- a proposal to determine the effects of weightlessness on people with circulatory diseases

- a proposal to test the feasibility of taking a pet into space

Expert Sources
- Dr. Lopez, child psychologist
- Dr. Malone, space medicine expert
- Dr. Zhang, veterinarian
- NASA report on space colonization by families
- NASA Research Report 342
- *New York Times*, a newspaper
- *Space Matters*, a journal
- *Space Medicine*, a journal
- UN Report on Families

PRACTICE 12

Choose a topic from the list to write a block-style contrastive essay. Use the chart to fill in the information to use in your support paragraphs before you begin your essay. Remember to write an introductory paragraph, support paragraphs that completely cover the first item before contrasting the second, and a clear conclusion.

TOPICS

- Black Holes vs. White Holes
- Two Kinds of Spacecraft
- A Gravity Environment vs. Weightlessness
- (your own idea)

Support Paragraph 1	Support Paragraph 2

YOU'RE IN CHARGE!

UNIT TEN OBJECTIVES: How well did you meet the objectives for this unit? Check the box next to each objective you feel you mastered.

GRAMMAR	LISTENING	SPEAKING
❑ Future progressive tense ❑ Future perfect tense	❑ Listening to interpret relationships between ideas	❑ Citing authoritative sources for support

PRONUNCIATION	READING	WRITING
❑ Rising-falling intonation to indicate new information	❑ Recognizing comparison and contrast examples	❑ Analyzing a block-style essay of comparison or contrast ❑ Writing a block-style essay of comparison or contrast

LEARNING STRATEGIES: Reflect on your use of learning strategies and thinking skills in this unit. What are some of the strategies you employed? Which ones were most successful for you?

Write your thoughts here.

_____

_____

_____

_____

_____

_____

_____

_____

_____

Unit 10 Learning Strategies

- Drawing conclusions
- Using prior knowledge
- Using context to determine meaning
- Making predictions
- Classifying
- Comparing and contrasting
- Working cooperatively
- Noting details
- Brainstorming

PRACTICE 1

Work in small groups to discuss these questions.

- What are your vacation habits?
- Do you usually travel or relax at home?
- What are the advantages and disadvantages of each?

PRACTICE 2

Use the words in the box to complete the sentences.

artifacts	immersed
figurine	stimulate
scenic	donate
dig	suspense

Iguazu Falls

1. Many people visit Iguazu Falls at the junction of Brazil, Argentina, and Paraguay. The falls are known for their _____ beauty.

2. I'm planning to go on a dinosaur _____ with my cousin this summer; we're really excited!

3. In Egypt, my friend bought a clay _____ representing Nefertiti.

4. There's nothing like white-water rafting to _____ your adrenalin and make you appreciate you're alive!

5. In preparation for my shipwreck dive, I _____ myself in reading about the history of the ship I would explore.

6. Our local sporting goods store is willing to _____ the equipment we need for the youth club camping trip so we won't have to buy it.

7. A number of valuable _____ disappeared from the recently discovered tomb.

8. You open the letter! I can't stand the _____! Was I accepted as a member of the expedition?

PRACTICE 3

A. Two travelers are waiting in line to check in at the airport. Work with a partner. Complete the conversation.

ROLES	CONVERSATION	FUNCTIONS
Traveler 1:	So where are you traveling to?	Ask a question.
Traveler 2:	I'm going horseback riding through Ireland, but I wish _____ _____.	Reply and express a wish.
Traveler 1:	Why is that?	Ask a follow-up question.
Traveler 2:	I'm afraid of horses. I wish I _____ _____.	Explain the circumstances behind your wish.

B. Take turns being the travelers and discuss other vacation plans.

VACATION PLANS	REASON	WISH
a. photo safari in Kenya	allergic to insects	visit a health spa
b. cave exploring in Belize	afraid of small spaces	be at the beach
c. dinosaur dig	hurt my back	stay home
d. shark fishing trip	get sea sick	go to the mountains

PRACTICE 4

A. Rewrite the sentences below as conditions, omitting *if* and using the verb in parentheses.

> **Example:** Ken hurt his foot, so he and his wife couldn't sign up for the hiking trip. **(had)**
> _Had Ken not hurt his foot, he and his wife would have signed up for the hiking trip._

1. Carrie missed her flight to Tokyo, and so she had to wait 14 hours for the next flight. **(had)**

   _____

   _____

2. Louis isn't careful. He lost his passport and traveler's checks. **(were)**

   _____

   _____

3. You probably won't go on the camping trip. But if you do go camping, you'll need water purification tablets. **(should)**

   _____

   _____

4. Jennifer didn't stay an extra day at the ski lodge, so she wasn't trapped there during the snowstorm. **(had)**

_____

_____

5. David isn't wearing good hiking boots, so he had to turn back. **(were)**

_____

_____

6. A shark probably won't swim by you. But if it does, you'll want to stay as still as possible. **(should)**

_____

_____

PRACTICE 5

On a separate sheet of paper, write sentences describing the wishes of the people in the pictures. Then compare your sentences with a partner's.

Example: _She wishes she knew how to ride a horse._

1.

2.

3.

4.

5.

6.

A. Complete the sentences with appropriate forms of the verbs in parentheses.

SYLVIA: I heard about your vacation, and I want all the details!

SARAH: The trip was a disaster from start to finish! Oh, I wish

I **(1. not/go)** _____!

SYLVIA: But why? You were so excited about your plans!

SARAH: If only I **(2. know)** _____, I **(3. stay)** _____

home. Why did I think I would enjoy two weeks at a cowboy ranch?

SYLVIA: Well, if I **(4. remember)** _____ correctly, you said

that you wished your life **(5. not/be)** _____ so predictable

and boring.

SARAH: I know. I even said I wished my vacation

(6. change) _____ my life. And it did—for the worse!

SYLVIA: Look, Sarah, anyone can get thrown off a wild horse!

SARAH: If it **(7. be)** _____ only that! I was actually glad to get off

the horse any way I could. I just wish it **(8. not/fall)** _____

on top of me and **(9. break)** _____ my arm!

SYLVIA: But you're lucky you escaped!

SARAH: Oh yeah. I just wish I **(10. not/run)** _____ through that

cactus patch to get away! It took two hours just to pull out the spines!

cactus patch

B. Work with a partner. Compare your answers and explain your choices.

PRACTICE 7

Each of the following people have certain regrets about decisions they made in life. Use the cues to write sentences using *if only*.

Example: I/finish college/get a better job
If only I had finished college! I would have gotten a better job by now.

1. Sue/remember to bring film/have great photos

   _____

   _____

2. Vera/learn to drive/be able to help on the safari

   _____

   _____

3. Nick/save money/go white water rafting

   _____

   _____

4. Bill/keep a first aid kit/handle the emergency

   _____

   _____

5. Pat/be less shy/have more fun on vacation

   _____

   _____

6. Maria/study archeology/lead the archeological dig

   _____

   _____

PRACTICE 8

A. **Before You Listen** Discuss with a partner. What are some of the especially memorable vacations you've taken? What was so special about them?

🎧 **B.** Listen to a conversation among friends and answer the questions.

1. Where did Ellen go for her vacation?

   _____

2. What kind of a vacation trip was it?

   _____

3. How long did the trip last?

   _____

4. What did Ellen do during her time underwater?

   _____

5. What did Ellen like best about the trip?

   _____

6. What did Yoko do for her vacation?

   _____

C. Listen again. Check the box that describes each speaker's tone.

ELLEN (the traveler)	**YOKO (first friend)**	**BOBBY (second friend)**
❏ upset	❏ angry	❏ curious
❏ curious	❏ envious	❏ sad
❏ excited	❏ sad	❏ upset

PRACTICE 9

A. Work with a partner. Read the paragraph and predict the thought groups. Mark vertical lines to separate the groups.

> One of the most beautiful places to explore caves is in Belize. In Cayo, you can cross rivers and hike through the jungle. You will reach a site where the ancient Mayan people held ritual ceremonies over 2000 years ago. The cave was discovered in 1989. It holds ceremonial vessels and other artifacts that reveal much about the Mayan civilization.

🎧 **B.** Listen to check your predictions.

C. Work with a partner and take turns reading the paragraph.

PRACTICE 10

Work in small groups. You and your partners are starting a new company to provide adventure vacation packages to travelers. Take turns discussing some of the possibilities for your new business venture. Use language from the box for providing support to other partners when appropriate.

VACATION PACKAGE POSSIBILITIES

- Underwater cave exploration
- Desert caravans along old trade routes
- Loch Ness monster searches
- Sea floor exploration trips
- Active volcano tours

> **Useful Language for Support**
>
> I think you have a valid point there.
> I'm throwing my weight behind . . .
> You've got my vote.
> That idea should be given our full consideration.
> Let's go with that solution.
> It seems right on target.
> I have to back (person's name) on this one.

PRACTICE 11

Choose two items from the list and brainstorm points to compare about them. Then write a block-style comparison essay with two support paragraphs.

cave exploration	mushroom hunting	shipwreck diving
exploring ruins	parasailing	skydiving
hunting safari	photo safari	kayaking
mountain climbing	sailing	white-water rafting

YOU'RE IN CHARGE!

Unit Eleven Objectives: How well did you meet the objectives for this unit? Check the box next to each objective you feel you mastered.

GRAMMAR
- ❑ Omitting *if* in conditional sentences
- ❑ Expressing wishes in the present, past, and future
- ❑ Using *if only* emphatically

LISTENING
- ❑ Listening to identify the tone of the speakers

SPEAKING
- ❑ Providing support during a discussion

PRONUNCIATION
- ❑ Identifying thought groups by pauses and intonation

READING
Recognizing comparisons and contrasts
- ❑ implicitly
- ❑ explicitly

WRITING
- ❑ Writing a block-style essay of contrast
- ❑ Using transition words to show contrast

Learning Strategies: Reflect on your use of learning strategies and thinking skills in this unit. What are some of the strategies you employed? Which ones were most successful for you?

Write your thoughts here.

_____

_____

_____

_____

_____

_____

_____

_____

_____

_____

Unit 11 Learning Strategies

- Drawing conclusions
- Using prior knowledge
- Using context to determine meaning
- Analyzing differences
- Making predictions
- Classifying
- Comparing and contrasting
- Working cooperatively
- Outlining
- Brainstorming

Unit 12

PRACTICE 1

Work in small groups and discuss these questions.

- What are some of the joys you have experienced in learning another language?
- What are some of the frustrations you have experienced in learning another language?
- What advice would you offer to a beginning language student?

PRACTICE 2

Complete the crossword puzzle. Refer to page 149 in your Student Book for help.

ACROSS

1. very funny
3. instance, example
6. hidden dangers
7. embarrassing word mistakes
8. burial place

DOWN

2. family from previous generations
4. confronted
5. product name tag
6. pie or baked dessert

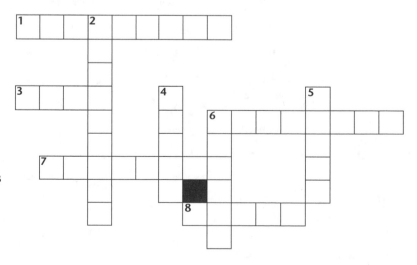

PRACTICE 3

A. Two students are discussing a speech their school principal gave.
Work with a partner. Practice the conversation.

ROLES	CONVERSATION	FUNCTIONS
Diana:	The school principal said we would be wearing uniforms next year.	Report what someone said.
Carlos:	What do you think he meant?	Ask for an interpretation.
Diana:	I think he meant that we could have a stronger school identity if we had a uniform.	Give an explanation.

B. Take turns with the roles below and discuss what other people said.

- **a.** ministers/what the president said
- **b.** coworkers/what the manager said
- **c.** teammates/what the coach said
- **d.** translators/what the author said
- **e.** journalists/what the expert said
- **f.** (your own idea)

PRACTICE 4

Read each numbered sentence and check the statement that best describes it.

1. La Rochefoucauld said, "It is more shameful to distrust one's friends than to be deceived by them."

   - ☐ La Rochefoucauld said that it had been more shameful to distrust your friends, but now it was better to deceive them.

   - ☐ La Rochefoucauld said that it was more shameful to distrust your friends than to be deceived by them.

2. "No one can make you feel inferior without your consent," Eleanor Roosevelt said.

   - ☐ Eleanor Roosevelt said that no one would make you feel inferior without your consent.

   - ☐ Eleanor Roosevelt said that no one could make you feel inferior without your consent.

3. Groucho Marx said, "I've had a marvelous evening, but this wasn't it."

   - ☐ Groucho Marx said that he had been a marvelous evening, but this wasn't it.

   - ☐ Groucho Marx said that he had had a marvelous evening, but this wasn't it.

PRACTICE 5

A. Write the following sentences in reported speech.

Gabriel García Márquez

1. "The Colombian novelist Gabriel García Márquez won the Nobel Prize for Literature in 1982."

   My friend said _____

   _____.

2. "Have you read any translations of Gabriel García Márquez's books?"

   I asked her _____.

3. "I'm reading the English translation of *Love in the Time of Cholera*."

   My friend replied _____.

4. "I hear Gabo, as he is fondly called, is writing his memoirs."

   I add _____.

5. "He will be publishing three volumes of memoirs in the near future."

   My friend remarked _____.

6. "Do you think we can find more information about García Márquez on the Internet?"

   I asked her _____.

B. Compare your sentences with a partner's and explain your use of reported speech.

PRACTICE 6

Work with a partner. Take turns telling each other in reported speech what the man and woman said.

assorted sushi

MR. WALKER:	Where do you want to eat today?
MS. CHAPLIN:	I love the Sushi Palace. Their sushi and sashimi are fabulous.
MR. WALKER:	I agree. And their prices are good too.
MS. CHAPLIN:	How do you translate sushi?
MR. WALKER:	I don't know, but it's raw fish on top of rice.
MS. CHAPLIN:	Have you tried their tempura?
MR. WALKER:	No, but I will. Which one do you recommend?
MS. CHAPLIN:	Last time I had shrimp tempura. It's their specialty!

PRACTICE 7

A. Before You Listen Work with a partner. What are some pitfalls you have experienced translating from one language to another? Are thoughts expressed exactly the same way from language to language?

B. Listen to friends talking about their experiences. Decide if the statements are **T** (true) or **F** (false).

_____ **1.** José has been to the United States on more than one occasion.

_____ **2.** José brought his bathing suit on a fishing trip.

_____ **3.** Julia tried to buy shampoo in Japan but had a problem.

_____ **4.** Tom visited Mexico and did some grocery shopping while he was there.

_____ **5.** The friends are sharing some experiences of being in a foreign culture.

C. Listen again. Work with a partner and answer these questions.

1. According to the conversation, what kind of experiences were the friends discussing?

_____

2. What language problem caused the confusion about "pool"?

_____

3. What language problem caused the confusion about "cocoa"?

_____

4. What language problem caused the confusion about "groceries"?

_____

5. What can happen to words and expressions when they are translated into another language?

_____

PRACTICE 8

A. Predict the rising-falling intonation in the following conversations. Draw an arrow ↑ above the words that express strong emotion.

                      ↑   ↑

Example: A: Hey! When did you get here, Toby?

               ↑ ↑

      B: Hi, Zachary! How are you? Oh, about ten minutes ago.

1. **A:** I got a raise!

   B: No!

   A: Yes! 350 dollars!

2. **A:** I'll get you a new computer when we can afford it.

   B: Sure!

   A: No, really!

3. **A:** Luther came in first!

   B: Right!

   A: I'm serious!

   B: Wow!

B. Listen to the conversations to check your predictions.

C. Work with a partner and take turns reading the conversations.

PRACTICE 9

A. Decide if the statements are **M** (managing time), **S** (summarizing the discussion), or **P** (previewing the next meeting).

_____ **1.** Considering the time that's left, could you keep your comments as brief as possible?

_____ **2.** We've gotten through four of the ten points today. Who would like to review them for us?

_____ **3.** So I think we could conclude that most of us feel foreign expressions enrich rather than threaten our language. Wonderful!

_____ **4.** All right. For next week, please have your budgets ready. We want to finalize plans for the coming year.

_____ **5.** We have just ten minutes left, so I will give you each two minutes to make any last comments.

B. Work in small groups. Discuss whether we should adopt foreign words and expressions into our languages or whether it's better to keep our languages as pure as possible. Take turns attending to time, summarizing the content of the discussion, and previewing the agenda for the next meeting.

YOU'RE IN CHARGE!

UNIT TWELVE OBJECTIVES: How well did you meet the objectives for this unit? Check the box next to each objective you feel you mastered.

GRAMMAR
- ❏ Statements in reported speech
- ❏ Questions in reported speech
- ❏ Using reporting verbs

LISTENING
- ❏ Listening to draw conclusions

SPEAKING
Closing a discussion
- ❏ Managing time
- ❏ Summarizing the discussion
- ❏ Previewing the next meeting agenda

PRONUNCIATION
- ❏ Rising-falling intonation to express emotion

READING
- ❏ Focusing on language choice and style

WRITING
- ❏ Self-editing
- ❏ Peer-editing

LEARNING STRATEGIES: Reflect on your use of learning strategies and thinking skills in this unit. What are some of the strategies you employed? Which ones were most successful for you?

Write your thoughts here.

_____

_____

_____

_____

_____

_____

_____

_____

_____

Unit 12 Learning Strategies
- Using prior knowledge
- Using context to determine meaning
- Noting main ideas
- Noting details
- Drawing conclusions
- Making predictions
- Comparing
- Analyzing
- Working cooperatively
- Brainstorming